1969 *Chevrolet* CHEVELLE SS 396

Dale McIntosh

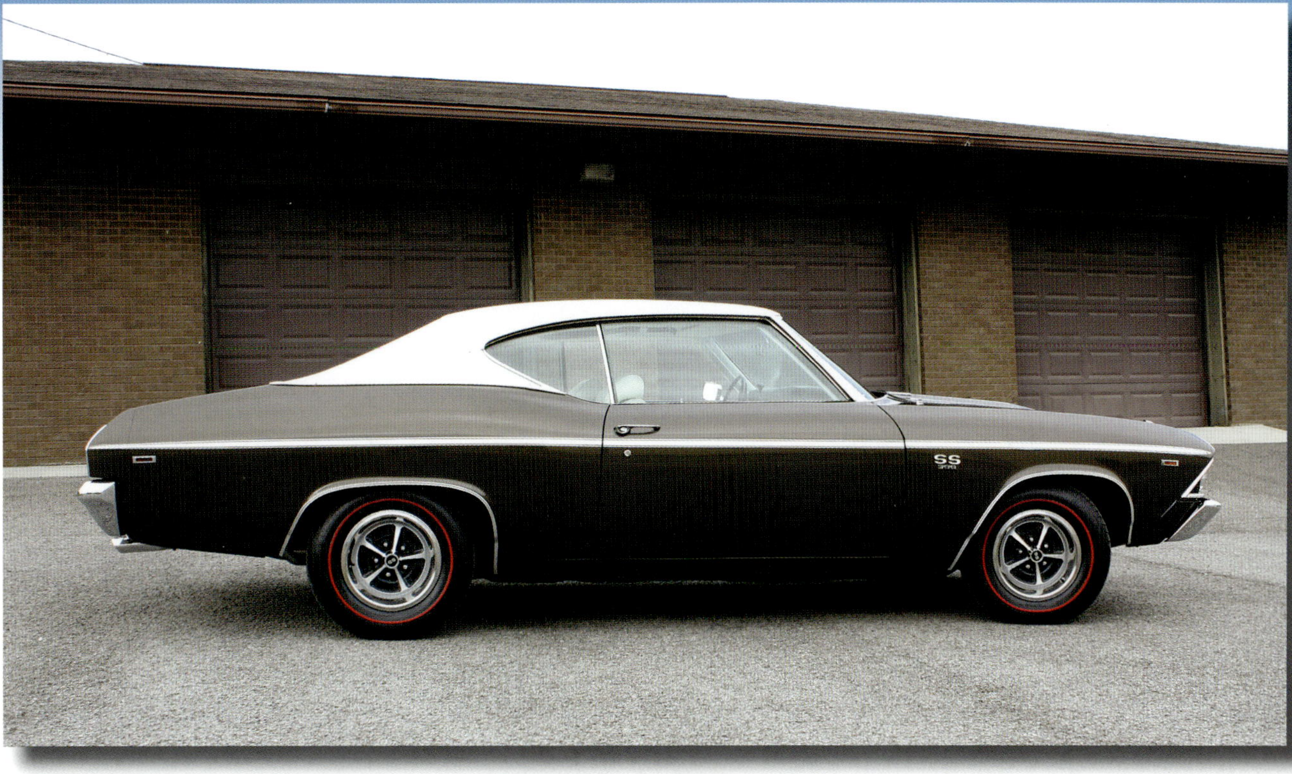

CarTech®

CarTech®, Inc.
838 Lake Street South
Forest Lake, MN 55025
Phone: 651-277-1200 or 800-551-4754
Fax: 651-277-1203
www.cartechbooks.com

Edit by Wes Eisenschenk
Layout by Connie DeFlorin

ISBN 978-1-61325-551-3
Item No. CT669

Library of Congress Cataloging-in-Publication Data Available

Written, edited, and designed in the U.S.A.
Printed in China
10 9 8 7 6 5 4 3 2 1

DISTRIBUTION BY:

Europe
PGUK
63 Hatton Garden
London EC1N 8LE, England
Phone: 020 7061 1980 • Fax: 020 7242 3725
www.pguk.co.uk

Australia
Renniks Publications Ltd.
3/37-39 Green Street
Banksmeadow, NSW 2109, Australia
Phone: 2 9695 7055 • Fax: 2 9695 7355
www.renniks.com

Canada
Login Canada
300 Saulteaux Crescent
Winnipeg, MB, R3J 3T2 Canada
Phone: 800 665 1148 • Fax: 800 665 0103
www.lb.ca

TABLE OF CONTENTS

ACKNOWLEDGEMENTS

This book would not have been possible without the support of many Chevelle enthusiasts and owners. They proofread this book for accuracy, spelling, and grammar, took photos of their cars, and shared memorabilia that is near and dear to them. Those individuals include Cliff Copeland, Donnie Edmonds, Chuck Frame, Sam Griffith, Dustin Herbison, Robert Killingsworth, Dave Krespan, Shawn McCurry, Russell Muller, Rick Nelson, Rocco Regina, Bill Rose, Les Savile, Shahreyar Shafei, Jeffrey Steffes, Todd Stewart, Christopher Toth, and Bill Whorley.

Those who donated materials and information as a commercial entity include Jo Marie Pitrolo of Anthony Chevrolet, Matthew Berger of Berger Chevrolet, the General Motors Media Archives, Rick Nelson of Musclecar Restoration & Design, Mecum Auctions, the L78 Registry, the Chevelle Registry, and the SS 396 Registry.

Technical consultants include Bill Lessenberry, Andy Martin, and Dan Vasic.

CHAPTER 1

INTRODUCING THE CHEVELLE

This 1964 Malibu SS sport coupe is Ermine White, the most popular color by sales with 69,006 1964 Chevelles painted this color. Note the Malibu SS–only 3-bar spinner full wheel covers that were part of the Malibu SS series. (Photo Courtesy Malibu SS Registry)

The 1969-model-year Chevelle was unveiled in late 1968, which followed the practice of each model year being released around September of the previous calendar year.

In national news, turmoil raged in the fall of 1968: there was unrest between Vietnam War protesters and the Illinois National Guard at the Democratic Nation Convention in Chicago, and feminists protested the Miss America Pageant in Atlantic City, New Jersey.

On the lighter side, The Beatles song "Hey Jude" was its first track released on the Apple label to the US, and it became the longest song (more than 7 minutes in length) to hit number one on Billboard's Hot 100 chart. In addition, Richard Nixon appeared on the TV show *Rowan & Martin's Laugh-In* to proclaim, "Sock it to me."

MALIBU SS: 1964–1965

Not only did Chevrolet enter the mid-size car market with the the Malibu SS in 1964 and 1965 but it was also a precursor of many other exciting models from Chevrolet. Any L6 or V-8 engine available in the Chevelle engine lineup was available in both the 1964 and 1965 Malibu SS–series sport coupes and convertibles. The L6 engine was only available in a Chevelle SS for two years: 1964 and 1965.

Pontiac Strikes First

The 1964 Pontiac Tempest with the G.T.O. option dominated the General Motors A-Body horsepower ratings with its 325-hp 4-barrel 389-ci V-8 and the 348-hp Tri-Power option. In 1965, ratings increased to 335 hp and to a whopping

A 1965 Malibu SS convertible is shown in Cameo Beige with a beige convertible top and the base 283-ci V-8 engine. In 1965, Malibu SS V-8 convertible sales were down to 9,128 units from 11,191 in their introductory year of 1964. (Photo Courtesy Bill Whorley)

360 hp with the Tri-Power option.

The Chevelle countered in late 1964 with the option of a 300-hp 327-ci V-8. In 1965, the Chevelle seriously took up the challenge with its 350-hp RPO (regular production option) L79.

A teaser for the Chevelle lineup to regain superiority in the horsepower wars within General Motors occurred when the displacement limit was raised to 400 ci in the midsize lineup. Chevrolet commissioned a special run of the now-legendary RPO Z16 Malibu SS 396. With its 396-ci V-8 and 375 hp on tap, the gauntlet had been thrown down. Although Chevrolet came up short in the displacement race to Buick's 401-ci V-8, the Chevelle was king of the horsepower war (for now). All production Malibu SS 396 Chevelle Sport Coupes were built at the Leeds assembly plant in Kansas City, Missouri, with very few options available. Color options were Regal Red, Tuxedo Black, and Crocus Yellow. Of those 200 production Chevelles, 175 were to be sold to customers, and 25 were assigned by public relations for press driving. An estimated 70 survive today, and more barn finds are being discovered.

The Competition: Grand Sport and 442

The Buick Grand Sport was an option on the 1965 Skylark, but it boasted the 325-hp 401-ci V-8, while the Oldsmobile 4-4-2 received a new 345-hp 400-ci V-8. The 4-4-2 nameplate originally stood for 4-barrel carburetor, 4-speed transmission, and dual exhaust in 1964, but it changed for 1965 to denote a 400-ci engine, 4-barrel carburetor, and dual exhaust. A 3-speed column-shifted manual was the base transmission, and optional transmissions were the 4-speed manual and the 2-speed Super Turbine 300 automatic.

SS 396: 1966–1968

In 1966, Chevrolet introduced the SS 396 series, which was initially only available in the sport coupe and convertible bodystyles. The SS 396 series continued

A 1966 SS 396 sport coupe is shown in the popular Madeira Maroon. It was the first year the SS 396 became a series separate from the 300, 300 Deluxe, and Malibu series and featured the new-for-1966 "strut back" roofline on SS 396s and Malibus.

through the 1968 model year. The only year for the SS 396 El Camino to be included in the SS 396 series was 1968, as noted by its vehicle identification number (VIN) designation of 13880.

1966

The first year of the SS 396 saw three engine options: the base 325-hp SS 396 engine, the optional 360-hp RPO L34, and the killer 375-hp RPO L78. The L78 was released to dealers in February 1966, but there was no public advertising until later. A heavy-duty 3-speed manual transmission was standard. Several Muncie 4-speed transmissions or the venerable Powerglide 2-speed automatic was behind the base 396 and the L34 engine option. The L78 engine could not be ordered with a Powerglide.

The only non-SS 396 bodystyle that was able to be ordered with any 396-ci engine was the El Camino. Both the 13480 300 Deluxe and 13680 Malibu series were able to be ordered with any 396 engine, but they were not SS 396-series Chevelles.

The Buick, Oldsmobile, and Pontiac divisions were playing along as well. The 1966 Pontiac G.T.O. was now its own series and no longer an option on the Tempest. The Oldsmobile 4-4-2 option had a new 400-ci V-8 rated at 350 hp and a Tri-Power setup that boasted 360 hp. The Buick Grand Sport was still an option on the Skylark, using the 401-ci V-8. However, it was listed as 400 ci in sales brochures to meet the General Motors limit of 400 ci in intermediate-sized cars.

1967

Aside from some styling changes, the 1967 SS 396 engine lineup was about the same as the 1966 SS 396. The 360-hp L34 engine was downgraded to 350 hp, and the new Turbo Hydra-matic 400 3-speed automatic transmission became available and could be ordered behind any 396 engine in 1967. The 375-hp L78 engine was initially dropped from the options list but returned with very little fanfare and essentially no advertising in April 1967. As

1969 Chevrolet Chevelle SS 396
In Detail No. 12

A 1967 SS 396 sport coupe is shown in Capri Cream and optioned with a black vinyl top. In 1967, it was the first year for the RPO M40 Turbo Hydra-matic 400 (TH400) 3-speed automatic transmission and disc brake options in the SS 396 Chevelle.

a result, only 612 L78 engine options were sold in 1967, and all were equipped with either the Muncie M20 or Muncie M21 manual 4-speed transmission. No 1967 L78 engines were sold with an automatic transmission.

Like the 1966 model year, the only non-SS 396 bodystyle that could be ordered with any 396 engine was the El Camino. Both the 13480 300 Deluxe and 13680 Malibu series were able to be ordered with any 396 engine but were not SS 396-series Chevelles. And, again like the 1966 model year, no El Camino ordered with a 396 engine came with the distinctive SS 396 features, such as the blacked-out grille treatment, SS faux-scooped hood, or (in the case of 1967) the SS 396-only black-crinkle-finished dash strip.

The Pontiac G.T.O. dropped the Tri-Power carburetor setup in favor of the Rochester Quadrajet 4-barrel carburetor. The engine displacement was increased to the GM corporate limit of 400. The Buick Grand Sport became its own series but still offered a variety of engines with the 401 V-8 as the top of the line. The Oldsmobile 4-4-2 continued to be an option on the Cutlass platform.

1968

The 1968 model year was the first and last year that the Chevelle SS 396 El Camino was a separate series along with the sport coupe and convertible. The same three 396 engines from the 1967 model year were available: the 325-hp

This is a 1968 SS 396 El Camino in Seafrost Green with the optional black vinyl top. This was the only year the SS 396 El Camino was its own series: 13880. The first year an optional wheel design was offered was 1968. Shown here are the optional ZJ7 rally wheels. (Photo Courtesy SS 396 Registry)

version was the base engine, and the 350-hp L34 and 375-hp L78 engines were optional. The 2-speed Powerglide continued to be an option behind the base L35 and optional L34 engines, but 1968 was the last year that the 2-speed Powerglide was offered behind a 396 engine in Chevelles. The heavy-duty manual 3-speed transmission remained standard fare, and three Muncie 4-speed transmissions as well as the TH400 automatic were optional.

1969

Several taglines were used for the 1969 Chevelle: "America's most popular midsize car," "Putting you first keeps us first," "Chevelles appeal to two age groups. Under 30. And Over," and "1969 Chevrolet Chevelle SS 396 Sport Coupe. Chevelle: The concentrated Chevrolet. Just add gas."

Only minor body and trim updates from 1968 were implemented for the 1969 model year. The taillamps were enlarged and extended up the rear quarter panel. The coupe, sport coupe, convertible, and sedan pickup retained the same wheelbase as the 1968 model year: 112 inches for the coupe, sport coupe, and convertible; and 116 inches for the sedan pickup.

The dash was redesigned from the 1968 model year. The square-shaped speedometer and gauge pods became round. The speedometer remained in the left pod, and a full-size fuel gauge and various warning lamps occupied the right pod. A smaller pod was centered over the steering column and incorporated the RPO U35 electric clock if it was ordered.

New for 1969 was a two-spoke steering wheel. While non-SS-optioned 1969 Chevelles received a color that coordinated the steering wheel with the interior, all SS-optioned cars were fitted with a black steering wheel regardless of the interior color. The exception was the RPO N34 wood-grained plastic steering wheel; it was available as an option on all 1969 Chevelles, so it was not an SS-specific option. The ignition switch moved from the dash to the steering column and incorporated a steering column lock mechanism that required an automatic transmission to be in *park* and a manual transmission to be in *reverse* before the ignition key could be removed.

SS EQUIPMENT OPTION: 1969

In 1969, the SS Equipment option became just that, an option under regular production option (RPO) code Z25, even though it was still commonly referred to and promoted as an SS 396. The 1969 model year was the only year that the SS Equipment option was able to be ordered in a series other than the Malibu series. The 1969 300 Deluxe coupe (13427) and 300 Deluxe sport coupe (13437) could be ordered with the SS Equipment options package.

The SS Equipment option was not an *upgrade* option on the 300 Deluxe or Malibu series. The SS Equipment package was an option (just like a radio, power steering, or air-conditioning was optional). The SS Equipment package included several items that were available separately to all other Chevelles, such as power disc brakes, but some items were unique to the SS Equipment option, such as special SS wheels and RPO F41 Special Suspension. Contrary to popular belief, RPO F41 Special Suspension was not standard with the SS Equipment option; it was optional

A 1969 SS Equipment–optioned Malibu convertible is shown here in LeMans Blue with the optional RPO D96 Accent Stripe and equipped with the optional 375-hp RPO L78 engine. It was one of five series/bodystyles with which the SS Equipment option was available. (Photo Courtesy L78 Registry)

The only year that any SS Equipment–optioned Chevelle was available in any series other than the Malibu series was 1969. Both the 300 Deluxe sport coupe and the 300 Deluxe pillared coupe, shown here in LeMans Blue, could order the SS Equipment option. (Photo Courtesy L78 Registry)

only with the SS Equipment option, but only 722 were ordered in 1969. The 1969 SS-optioned Chevelle was the first year that any SS came standard with its own special wheels. These wheels were not optional on any non-SS-optioned Chevelle, and there were no optional wheel covers available for SS-optioned Chevelles.

Since this book deals with 1969 Chevelles that were ordered with the SS Equipment option (RPO Z25 with the 396/402-ci engine), only specific data on the coupe, sport coupe, convertible, and sedan pickup bodystyles with this option are listed. Exterior paint colors, interiors, rear-end gear ratios, some transmissions, and many options were available on non-SS-optioned Chevelles as well (with the exception of two colors that were a regular production option on SS Equipment–optioned Chevelles only).

Engine Options

For the 1969 model year, the SS 396 become an option instead of being the separate series that it was in 1966, 1967, and 1968. The SS Equipment option (RPO Z25) used essentially the same 396 engine as previous years. The 325-hp 396 was the base engine, and the 350-hp RPO L34 and 375-hp RPO L78 were optional. New for the 1969 Chevelle was an aluminum cylinder head option (RPO L89). The aluminum-head option was only available with the 375-hp L78 engine but (strangely) did not affect the advertised horsepower. The option took about 60 pounds of weight off the front end. Tonawanda engine plant numbers indicate that 412

aluminum-head RPO L89 options were built for 1969: 400 were sold and 12 were used for service engines.

Transmission Options

Numerous automatic transmission options were offered in Chevelles. The Powerglide 2-speed automatic was available from 1964 through 1973. A 3-speed Turbo Hydra-matic 350 (the TH350 and later variants) was first introduced in the 1969 model year and was available through 1977. A beefier Turbo Hydra-matic 400 (TH400) was first used in Chevelles in 1967 and was only available behind the 396/402 engine in 1969.

Several manual 3-speed transmissions were installed in Chevelles. Various light-duty and heavy-duty 3-speed manual and 3-speed manual overdrive transmissions saw duty with all Chevelle engines except the 396 or 427 in 1969. It may be surprising to some, but the heavy-duty 3-speed was the standard transmission that was used in the SS 396 series from 1966 to 1968 and the SS Equipment–optioned Chevelles in 1969. Various gear ratios for first, second, and reverse were used depending on the year and engine that was ordered. The last model year for a manual floor-shifted 3-speed transmission as standard equipment with the SS Equipment option was 1969.

Several manual 4-speed transmissions were offered as options throughout the years. What is commonly called a wide-ratio or wide-range 4-speed was first offered in 1964 and was also used in 1965. The RPO code for this transmission is M20. This RPO code became important

in mid-1966. The 1964 and 1965 versions of the Muncie M20 differed from later versions in several ways; gear ratios were most apparent. The 1964 and 1965 Muncie M20 has a first-gear ratio of 2.56:1, a second-gear ratio of 1.91:1, a third-gear ratio of 1.48:1, and (of course) fourth gear was 1.00:1. Reverse was 2.64:1. The 1966-and-later Muncie M20 4-speed transmissions changed the ratios to a first-gear ratio of 2.52:1, a second-gear ratio of 1.88:1, a third-gear ratio of 1.46:1, and fourth gear remained the same at 1.00:1. The reverse gear ratio changed to 2.59:1.

Sometime around February or March 1966, Chevelles were introduced to a second wide-ratio 4-speed transmission. A cast-iron case unit was built at the Saginaw, Michigan, transmission plant and was typically used behind engines of 300 hp or less. This Saginaw 4-speed carried the same RPO number: M20. When a dealer or individual buyer ordered a Chevelle with a 4-speed, the dealer checked the *4-speed wide range* box. When the order

reached the assembly plant, the car would receive the aluminum Muncie M20 or the cast-iron Saginaw M20. The gear ratios in the Saginaw 4-speed manual transmissions varied depending on the engine.

All automatic and manual transmissions were supposed to have a VIN derivative stamped on them, but that has been shown to not be the case (many Chevelle transmissions have been documented without a VIN derivative stamped on them). Typically, the engine and transmission were stamped with the VIN derivative at the time the two were mated, so the fonts of the characters should be the same size and type. The Flint and Tonawanda engine assembly plant VIN derivative stamps vary date and suffix code stamps in terms of size and font style because they were stamped at different facilities.

SS-only Paint Options

Both RPO code 926PP for Daytona Yellow (paint code 76 on a trim tag) and RPO code 927QQ for Hugger/Monaco Orange (paint code 72 on a trim tag) were

This 1969 SS Equipment–optioned Malibu sport coupe has one of two special SS Equipment-option-only colors: Hugger Orange. The special SS-only colors Hugger Orange and Daytona Yellow were still a $42.15 option. (Photo Courtesy SS 396 Registry)

only available under those RPO codes on SS Equipment–optioned Chevelles but were still an extra $42.15. These two colors were available on any other 1969 Chevelle under RPO ZP3 Special Paint at an additional cost.

Some 1969 SS 396 Chevelle fans call the orange *Hugger Orange*, and some refer to it as *Monaco Orange*. It is the same color. Some aftermarket paint chip charts (such as PPG) show paint code 72 as *Hugger Orange* under the general Chevrolet banner but as a Camaro color and *Monaco Orange* as the Corvette color. An internal General Motors document that showed the production total of Chevelle colors referred to the color orange with the sales name of *Hugger Orange*. Be aware that Hugger Orange, Monaco Orange, Daytona Yellow, and others are all sales names—just like Fathom Green, Garnet Red, or LeMans Blue are sales names used by Chevrolet. Internally, General Motors simply refers to these colors as dark green, red, and bright blue. So, whether you prefer to call it Hugger Orange or Monaco Orange, it's just orange to Chevrolet.

These two SS-only colors were still an option for any other 1969 Chevelle, but they would have to be ordered through what General Motors called a Fleet & Special Order (F&SO) system. Virtually any color available at the time could have been ordered: a General Motors, Ford, or Mopar color, or even any color from an OEM paint supplier. A special-order paint color costed up to $125, depending on the color and queued production run of that color. Typically, the F&SO system was used for fleet cars for government agencies and companies that purchased fleet of cars and wanted them in a special color, but the system was available to individuals as well. The buyer needed to tell (and often convince) the salesperson to place the order with the selected color. Normally, when a special-order paint code was placed, the assembly plant identified the paint code on the Fisher Body number plate (the trim tag or cowl tag) with either a dash or hyphen character (-). If the color was available on other 1969 General Motors models, sometimes the assembly plant used the paint code for the color on the applicable model or the F&SO number.

Special Paint

Codes, such as B1699 for 1969 Camaro Rallye Green, have been found along with B1958 on Baltimore-built 1969 Chevelles. It is unknown why Baltimore used the F&SO code on some Fisher Body number plates and a dash or hyphen on others.

See the appendix for more details on 1969 Chevelle paint codes.

The Buick, Oldsmobile, and Pontiac divisions of General Motors had their own A-Body platform cars. Buick had the Skylark nameplate, Oldsmobile had the Cutlass, and Pontiac had the LeMans. Buick, Oldsmobile, and Pontiac also had various trim levels and specialty models. The top dogs in performance were the Buick GS, Oldsmobile 4-4-2, and Pontiac GTO.

Each General Motors division had its own design and engineering departments, and there was very little common-

ality between them. They had different engine designs, interior designs, and more. Many transmissions were essentially the same, such as the Muncie 4-speed and TH400.

Although some variations in paint colors were offered, often the same paint color and mixing formula had a different sales name. For example, the 1969 Chevelle white was called *Dover White*. Buick called this same color *Polar White*, and to Oldsmobile and Pontiac buyers, it was *Cameo White*.

THE COMPETITION

GM A-Body muscle cars outsold Chrysler at a ratio of about 4:1, even though the Dodge and Plymouth divisions had powerful muscle cars of their own, including the B-Body Belvedere, GTX, Coronet, and more with the 383-/426-/440-ci Wedge and 426 Hemi. To capture more of the youth market that was buying muscle cars, Plymouth devised a low-budget muscle car based on the Belvedere model with some trick graphics and marketing that resulted in the Road Runner. The only real competition on the marketing end for General Motors was the G.T.O. Judge, an attempt to cash in on the comedy routine "Here come da judge" from the Rowan & Martin *Laugh-In* TV show. The Judge was to be a low-cost G.T.O., but it was actually more expensive than a standard G.T.O. However, it included the Ram Air IV engine, spoiler, T-shaped Hurst-controlled 4-speed and vivid graphics.

Here is an SS Equipment–optioned 1969 Malibu sport coupe in LeMans Blue with the optional RPO D96 Accent Stripe, a $26.35 option, available only on an SS Equipment–optioned Chevelle. Like the rear tail panel, the grille was blacked out except for the bright top, center, and bottom horizontal bars. (Photo Courtesy SS 396 Registry)

CHAPTER 2

DESIGN AND CONCEPT

The vents in the upper firewall cowl area were part of the new Astro Ventilation that allowed greater passenger comfort and improved ventilation and air distribution.

In 1968 and 1969, the Chevelle (often called Gen 3 because it is the third major bodystyle) took on a new look from previous years with tapered front fenders, sharper-defined front fascia, and new chassis dimensions.

The 1969-model-year body lines and trim were more of a refinement of the 1968 design than a radical change, much like how 1965 model year was a refinement of 1964 and how the 1967 model year was a refinement of 1966. However, several features were introduced with the 1969 model year. Both sport coupes (the 13437 series 300 Deluxe and 13637 Malibu) as well as the Malibu-series convertible received a one-piece front side glass, and these three models eliminated the vent wing for driver and passenger in favor of "Astro Ventilation."

ASTRO VENTILATION

The idea was to have outside air enter the cabin from the cowl vents on top of the firewall through the dash and kick panels and exit into the trunk. The air then circulates forward into the quarter panels and exits through the black vents in the doorjambs. Astro Ventilation has nothing to do with the RPO C60 air-conditioning option. As noted, only the two sport coupes (300 Deluxe series and Malibu series) and the Malibu-series convertible bodystyles were so equipped; all other bodystyles retained the vent windows for driver and front passenger.

HIDEAWAY WINDSHIELD WIPERS

All Malibu and Concours station wagon series in 1969 featured hideaway windshield wipers, while the lesser Nomad and 300 Deluxe series did not. Available as an option with the Nomad and 300 Deluxe series was hideaway windshield wipers, but only 706 buyers opted for RPO C24. The rear of the hood had a small turn-up to help conceal the wiper arms/blades, and the lower windshield trim was wider on the Malibu and Concours series so that the wiper arms could *park* below the rear of the hood opening. When a 300 Deluxe coupe (13427) or a 300 Deluxe sport coupe (13437) was ordered with the SS 396 Equipment option, part of the option on those two Chevelle models was hideaway windshield wipers and the SS scooped hood.

The cowl vents did not have covers. In many parts of the country, it was soon discovered that paper, leaves, critters, and other debris was easily trapped in the cowl vents, so someone came up with a product to combat this: the cowl vent grille screen. These are readily available in the aftermarket even today.

EL CAMINO

The sedan pickup (commonly known and marketed as the *El Camino*) is as much of a Chevelle as the sport coupe or convertible; it's just a different bodystyle. Somewhere along the evolutionary path, in the mindset of many, the sedan pickup

Critters and debris often found their way into the cowl vents, which led many owners (and probably dealers as well) to install aftermarket grates over the vents to alleviate the issue and provide some peace of mind. (Photo Courtesy L78 Registry)

The Malibu-series El Camino is one of five 1969 Chevelle models that one could order with the SS 396 Equipment option. An *el Camino* nameplate replaced the *Chevelle by Chevrolet* on the header panel. (Photo Courtesy Bill Rose)

lost its identity as a Chevelle. In aftermarket parts catalogs, Chevelle car clubs, etc. you will see something like "Chevelle and El Camino." One never sees "Chevelle and Greenbrier" or "Chevelle and convertible." The sedan pickup (El Camino) is just one of the several bodystyles in the entire Chevelle lineup.

There were some options that one could not get on the sedan pickup that one could get on a sport coupe or sedan. An obvious option was rear seat belts, but there were options that one could not get on almost any bodystyle that one could get on another. How may convertibles have you seen with a power rear tailgate window? How may sport coupes have you seen with a power folding top? While the

sedan pickup is as much of a Chevelle as any of the bodystyles, it is often relegated to red-headed stepchild status, and that is a shame. Yes, the El Camino features a longer wheelbase than the sport coupe and convertible (116 inches versus 112 inches), but so do all station wagons and all four-door models, and they are still considered Chevelles.

SS 396

The sedan pickup came in both the 300 Deluxe and Malibu series, but unlike the 300 Deluxe coupe and 300 Deluxe sport coupe, only the Malibu-series sedan pickup was a candidate for the SS 396 Equipment option. The same SS

396 Equipment engine and transmission options offered on other bodystyles were available on the sedan pickup. The same exterior paint colors were available. Naturally, there were some minor exterior trim differences between the sedan pickup and, say, the sport coupe. The Malibu-series sedan pickup has a blacked-out insert on the tailgate when equipped with the SS 396 Equipment option, and a centered SS 396 emblem tells all. New for the 1969 sedan pickup were the backup lamps on the tailgate and rear side marker lamps.

The sedan pickup (along with several other bodystyles) retained its vent windows, and sedan pickups continued to incorporate them over the one-piece front side windows found in the sport coupes and convertibles. The parking and backup lamps in the rear bumper from the 1968 model year were replaced with simple reflectors.

Only three interior color schemes were available in the sedan pickup: black, blue, and saddle.

The same trim code, such as 755 for black bench seat or 756 for black bucket seat, was used for all Chevelles for which that interior was available. The sedan pickup had one unique interior code: 771 saddle bucket seats were sedan-pickup exclusive.

CLAY AND PROTOTYPE MOCK-UPS

Apparently General Motors was considering some type of fresh-air cowl-induction hood for the 1969 model year. This single domed hood shows an opening for a fresh-air induction system

A non-SS 396 Equipment-optioned El Camino has a wood-grain insert on the tailgate with a *Chevrolet* script emblem, but when optioned with the SS 396 Equipment option, the wood-grain insert was blacked-out and an *SS 396* emblem used. (Photo Courtesy Bill Rose)

and what appears to be a 396 script on the dome that would not make its appearance until the 1970 model year. It's odd that a mock-up would include an option such as RPO U46 Lamp Monitoring system, but it is there. Also, note the application of the RPO D96 Accent Stripe that also made the production cut. The Chevelle script nameplate on the header panel is sans the additional "By Chevrolet" portion of the emblem. Unfortunately, the General Motors Media Archive has a very small sample of 1969 Chevelle SS 396 photos.

Various rear taillamp and bumper treatments were considered. A dual rear taillamp design very similar to the 1968/1969 Beaumont built in Canada was considered. The left portion of the

A functional cowl-induction hood is an item that did not make the cut for 1969 and did not appear until the 1970 model year. Two items here that made it are the continued option of RPO U46 Light Monitoring System and SS-only RPO D96 Side Stripe. (Photo Courtesy of General Motors Media)

What made the cut for the 1969 SS 396 Equipment–optioned Chevelle was the raised, twin faux hood scoops with chrome-plated rear vents on each scoop.

1969 Chevrolet Chevelle SS 396
In Detail No. 12

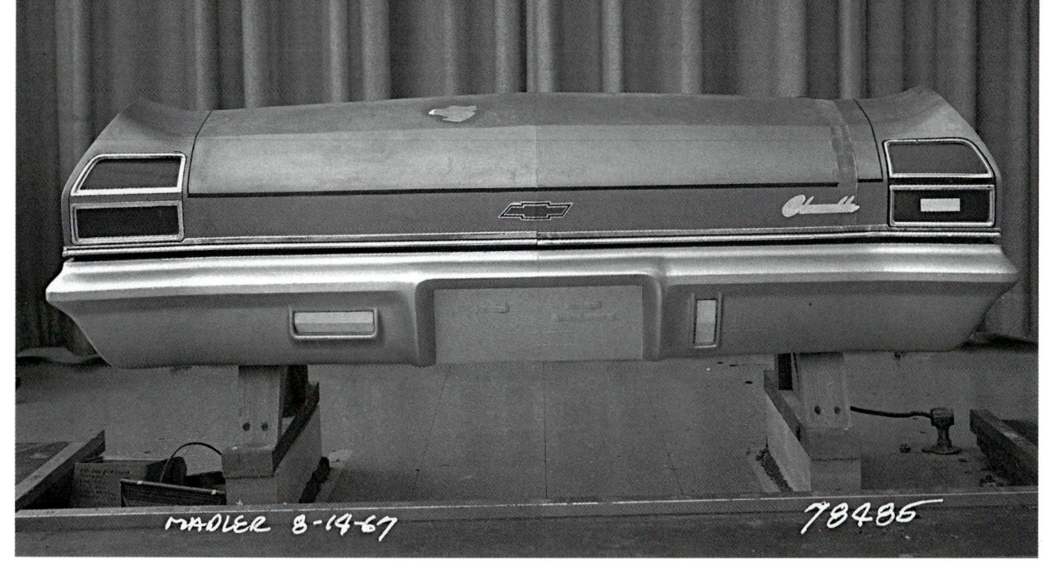

Variations of possible rear panel and taillamp treatments are shown. Note the three different backup lamp locations and configurations with photo date of August 19, 1967. (Photo Courtesy of General Motors Media Archive)

mock-up shows a horizontal backup lamp in the bumper, while the right portion shows both a backup lamp in the lower taillamp and a smaller vertical lamp on the bumper.

EXTERIOR SS 396 IDENTIFICATION

Overall styling changes were minor from the 1968 model year. The 1969 SS

On all Malibu and 300 Deluxe SS 396 Equipment–optioned sport coupes and convertibles, the rear tail panel was blacked out with bright trim top and bottom. The 300 Deluxe coupe and sport coupe were upgraded to the same taillamp housing as the Malibu.

396 grille retained its blackout theme along with an "SS 396" badge centered horizontally on the grille. Where the 1968 grille only has bright horizontal bars at the top and bottom edges, the 1969 model year added a single, wide horizontal bright bar and retained the wrap-around grille extensions, also blacked out except for the center rib. Trim no longer extended below the lower grille line and down the side of the car. Instead, it stopped at the lower grille line. The lower body color was now a continuous lower body color and not blacked out below the now-nonexistent side trim as the 1968 SS 396 was. The SS 396 Equipment option included a new SS 396 badge on the front fender behind the wheel opening. The year 1968 was the last year that standard steel wheels with hubcaps or optional full wheel covers were available on an SS 396 Chevelle. The 1969 SS 396 Equipment option included stylish Magnum 500 wheels, and no optional wheel covers were available. The front side marker was taken from the 300 Deluxe series and featured an amber lens with a clear bulb.

The front fender and lower body trim on the non-SS 396 Equipment-optioned 1969 Malibu sport coupe and convertible were similar to the 1968 model year. Where the 1968 SS 396 was painted black, the 1969 Malibu was Argent Silver.

1969 Chevrolet Chevelle SS 396
In Detail No. 12

Front Parking Lamps

Front parking/turn lamps were moved to larger openings in the bumper and were clear lenses with amber bulbs. The SS 396 Equipment option also included a bright trim ring around the parking/turn lamp lens regardless of series (Malibu or 300 Deluxe) or bodystyle (coupe, sport coupe, convertible, or sedan pickup). The non-SS 396 Equipment-optioned Malibu has a bright lower rocker molding with the lower side painted in Cortez Silver and no bright trim ring around the parking/turn lamps.

SS 396 EQUIPMENT OPTION

The SS 396 Equipment option for 1969 replaced the SS 396 series under RPO code Z25 and could be ordered with the Malibu-series sport coupe, convertible, and sedan pickup (and the 300 Deluxe–series coupe and 300 Deluxe–series sport coupe for 1969 only).

When RPO Z25 was ordered, the engine size designation was eliminated from the front side marker lamp and replaced with an *SS 396* emblem on the rear of the front fenders regardless of series or model. (Photo Courtesy L78 Registry)

The Malibu series has a longer trim piece extending down from the grille and matching the horizontal trim down the body with the lower portion of the body area done in Argent Silver. Note that the side marker incorporates the engine size when an optional L6 or any V-8 was ordered.

The extended trim from the headlamps and down the lower rocker panel from the Malibu was eliminated as well as the Argent Silver lower rocker panel color. Parking lamps for the SS 396 Equipment option have a bright metal ring around the lens.

The 300 Deluxe and Malibu series sport a blue bowtie in the center of the grille. The Malibu sports a longer headlamp molding that blends into the lower body panel, and the lower body panel is painted in Argent Silver. The non-SS-optioned 300 Deluxe and Malibu do not have bright trim around the front park/turn lamps.

An SS-optioned 300 Deluxe and Malibu had an *SS 396* emblem in the center of the grille. An SS-optioned Chevelle. has a bright trim ring around the front park/ turn lamps along with the 300 Deluxe–style side marker lamp.

1969 Chevrolet Chevelle SS 396
In Detail No. 12

The SS 396 Equipment package was an option like any other option, such as power steering, air-conditioning, a radio, etc. As such, the SS 396 Equipment package would not be noted in the VIN or on the trim tag of any 1969 Chevelle built in the United States.

Engine

The SS 396 Equipment option kept the same engine horsepower ratings from 1968. The 325-hp RPO L35 engine remained the base engine with the optional RPO L34 with 350 hp and RPO L78 with 375-hp engines available.

Transmission

A heavy-duty manual 3-speed floor-shifted transmission remained the base transmission for the SS 396 Equipment option with the three 4-speed manual transmissions and the 3-speed TH400 automatic as options. Gone from the SS 396 Equipment options list was the 2-speed Powerglide automatic transmission as an option, although the Powerglide remained for the 6-cylinder engines as well as the 307 V-8 and all 350 V-8s.

Cowl Tag

The Oshawa, Ontario, plant included some options on its trim tags so that any notation of L35 or L34 indicated the SS 396 option (but only for Canadian-built 1969 Chevelles). Many believe that Kansas City- and Baltimore-built SS 396 Equipment–optioned Chevelles have the letter *L* on a Malibu or 300 Deluxe trim tag below the lower paint code number, but there is no solid, irrefutable proof of the claim. There is strong circumstantial evidence that one can use to determine whether a 1969 SS 396 Equipment–optioned Chevelle is from the Kansas City or Baltimore plant. There have been several documented SS 396 Equipment Chevelles built at the Kansas City plant

Since the SS 396 Equipment was now an option and not its own series, the Fisher Body number plate did not immediately identify a Chevelle with this option. It is fairly certain that the Kansas City assembly plant used the letter *L* below the lower paint code to identify the body changes required.

SS 396 Equipment–optioned Chevelles built in Oshawa, Ontario, can readily be identified by the RPO code L35 or L34 on the third line just after the body assembly date (Photo Courtesy SS 396 Registry)

without the letter *L* on the trim tag. It's not common, but they do exist.

Chevelles built at the Oshawa, Ontario, plant in 1969 tell a different story. When one was ordered with the SS 396 Equipment option, several RPO codes will be shown on the Fisher Body number plate. Two of the three 396 engine codes (L35 or L34) will be stamped along with RPO code B79 for "Exterior Ornamentation Rear End" after January.

Vintage Vehicle Services in Oshawa, Ontario, can supply verification of a Chevelle that was built in Canada or originally sold in Canada that shows the car's options and build information. Most Canadian-imported Chevelles were built in Baltimore.

Bench Versus Bucket Seats

A cloth/vinyl bench seat was still standard for the Malibu sport coupe. The Malibu convertible and sedan pickup standard bench seat was all vinyl. Bucket seats were not part of the SS 396 Equipment option and could have been ordered in any Malibu-series sport coupe, convertible, or sedan pickup, but bucket seats could not have been ordered with the 300 Deluxe–series coupe or sport coupe even when the SS 396 Equipment option was.

Documentation from Vintage Vehicle Services on Canadian-built Chevelles initially sold in Canada is available for a fee and lists original options on the Chevelle. On this example, RPO B79 is called out along with RPO L34 and RPO Z25. (Photo Courtesy SS 396 Registry)

SHIPPING DATE:	February 5, 1969
MODEL NUMBER:	13637 – Malibu 2dr sport coupe
ENGINE:	396 CID 350 HP 4bbl Turbo
ENGINE NUMBER:	T0120JC
DEALER:	Chibougamau Auto Ltd. Chibougamau, PQ
NUMBER PRODUCED FOR SALE IN CANADA: (SAME MODEL NO. ONLY)	9, 612 (903 with Z/25; 294 with L/34)

OPTION	DESCRIPTION
A51	SEAT: FRONT BUCKET
B22	DOOR TRIM PAD EMBLEM
B79	EXTERIOR ORNAMENTATION REAR END
C08	EXTERIOR SOFT TRIM ROOF COVER
J50	BRAKES: VACUUM POWER
J52	BRAKES: FRONT DISC
L34	ENGINE: 396 CID TURBO JET V8
M20	TRANSMISSION: 4-SPEED MANUAL - WIDE RATIO
N40	POWER STEERING
PL5	TIRE: F70-14-4 PR - HWY - OE - B/WALL WHITE LETTERING
W84	ADDITIONAL FUEL FOR DELIVERY
ZKQ	TIRE PRESSURE LABEL
Z25	SUPER SPORT 396 PACKAGE
Z49	MANDATORY CANADIAN BASE EQUIPMENT MODIFICATIONS

1969 Chevrolet Chevelle SS 396
In Detail No. 12

The 300 Deluxe–series coupe and sport coupe retained their normal bench seat configuration and color availability.

There were no layout differences in the dash or instrument/warning lamp arrangement for an SS 396 Equipment–optioned Chevelle over any non-SS 396 Equipment–optioned Chevelle. There is a lot of misconception about the optional gauges offered. Even SS 396 Equipment–optioned Chevelles only came with a fuel gauge and speedometer as standard fare; other gauges and the clock were optional.

There is no such thing as "SS gauges." Since the 1966 model year, a tachometer and functional gauges were optional. All 1969 Chevelles came standard with a speedometer and fuel gauge; they also had warning lamps for water temperature, the alternator, and oil pressure.

RPO U14: Special Instrumentation

The Special Instrumentation option (RPO U14) consisted of a tachometer, electric water-temperature gauge, ammeter gauge, and an electric oil-pressure gauge in lieu of warning lamps. RPO U14 could have been ordered with any V-8 300 Deluxe coupe or sport coupe as well as any V-8 Malibu sport coupe, convertible, or sedan pickup. The only difference in the various U14 options was the redline of the tachometer. The 307-, 327-, and 350-ci engines redlined at 5,000 rpm, the L35 and L34 396-ci engines redlined at 5,500 rpm, and the L78 396-ci engine redlined at 6,000 rpm. The oil pressure, ammeter, and water-temperature gauges remained the same for each engine. RPO U14 also included the electric clock,

although it was also available as a separate option under RPO U35.

When RPO U14 was ordered (SS or not), the overall layout changed only slightly. A standard (non-gauge) dash has the speedometer/odometer in the left-most pod along with the parking brake lamp. The center pod has a filler plate with "CHEVELLE" script, and the right pod has a fuel-level gauge and warning lamps for water temperature, oil pressure, and the generator in a clockwise order. If the electric-clock option was ordered under RPO U35, it was located in the smaller, center pod. The RPO U14 Special Instrumentation option only changed the contents of the right pod. The fuel-level gauge remained at the 12 o'clock position and was now the same size as the water temperature, oil pressure, and battery gauge indicators, and a tachometer occupied the center section of the right pod. Since the electric clock was now part of the Special Instrumentation option, it was located in the small center pod. On a non-console-optioned Chevelle SS with the TH400 automatic transmission, the shift indicator was located just below the center pod. When a console was ordered with bucket seats, the TH400 shift mechanism moved to the floor, and the shift pattern was incorporated into the console.

RPO D96: Accent Striping

The RPO D96 Accent Striping option was only available when the SS 396 Equipment option was ordered and not available on any non-SS 396 Equipment–optioned Chevelle. See chapter 4 for accent stripe color choices.

CHAPTER 3

MARKETING AND PROMOTION

Chevrolet dealers offered all kinds of promotional items and accessories in their parts departments. This U-S-A–1 front plate promotes "Putting You First . . . Keeps Us First." (Photo Courtesy Chris Toth)

"Win on Sunday, Sell on Monday" was the mantra of the day and (to a fashion) remains today in professional racing. While one cannot go to his or her local Chevrolet, Ford, or Toyota dealer and buy a race car, brand loyalty is still alive and well. Chrysler, Ford, and Chevrolet are marketing high-performance Challengers, Mustangs, and Camaros, even producing limited editions of factory-backed race cars. Toyota is following suit by replacing its Camry in NASCAR with the new Supra and introducing it with a 335-hp street version. General Motors was well represented in the past, as NASCAR fielded entries from not only Chevrolet but also Buick, Oldsmobile, and Pontiac. However, by 2005, only Chevrolet remained.

THE MUSCLE CAR ERA

Although General Motors banned midsize cars with big engines, Pontiac's chief engineer John DeLorean and staff had an idea to transform Pontiac to a truly high-performance division of General Motors with the sly introduction of the G.T.O. option. Pontiac's boss Elliott "Pete" Estes got around GM's ban on big engines by offering the G.T.O. as mere $295.90 option for the A-Body Tempest. The G.T.O. option included the 389-ci 325-hp V-8 engine with a Hurst-shifted manual 3-speed with sport suspension, wider wheels, G.T.O. badging, dual exhaust, and a special non-functional scooped hood.

The 1964 G.T.O. is widely recognized as the first model to make the term *muscle car* a reality. It's a term that, arguably, could go back to the 1949 Oldsmobile with its Rocket V-8 or Chrysler's 300 series and its 300-hp Hemi V-8, but the term *muscle car* for the US market had not been used until the introduction of the G.T.O. for a small car–big engine combination. However, that's a discussion for another day.

In 1969, General Motors still had a ban on engines over 400 ci in its A-Body lineup. Chevrolet, Pontiac, Buick, and Oldsmobile were well into marketing to capture the youth market's dollars. Chevrolet had its old standby, the SS 396; Pontiac's G.T.O. and Judge option was alive and well with its 400-ci engine; Buick's GS400 had its 401-ci engine; and Oldsmobile had the 442 and its 400-ci engine. Unlike today, each division offered tons of individual options to suit the buyer's taste. The packaged options groups that we see today were rare (with the exception of such packages as auxiliary lighting or convenience items grouped together). Automatic versus manual transmissions, hood scoops, forced-air hoods, tachometer and gauges, several engine combinations, and special striping set the brands apart. Not only were performance goodies offered but also many special suspension packages were offered as well as some appearance options, such as spoilers from Buick and Oldsmobile.

Sales boomed in 1969 with Chevrolet's SS 396 sales at 86,307 units, Pontiac's G.T.O. sales at 72,287 units (6,833 optioned with the Judge package), and Oldsmobile's 442 sales at 27,263 units. Buick's GS400 sales lagged behind with just 7,532 units sold.

The Super Sport and SS nameplates have been a part of Chevrolet's promotional goodie bag since late 1961 with the introduction of the SS option on the full-size Impala. The Impala SS has been an on-again, off-again model ever since. The SS nameplate has shown up on the Cobalt, HHR (Heritage High Roof), Impala, and even the SSR (Super Sport Roadster). The Chevelle series has had some form of SS from its beginnings in 1964 through 1973: the 1964 and 1965 model years have their Malibu SS series; the 1966–1968 model years saw the SS 396 as its own series; in 1969, the SS Equipment package became a regular production option under RPO Z25; 1970 saw RPO Z25 for the SS 396 and RPO Z15 for the SS454; and 1971 and 1972 had the RPO Z15 relegated back to simply an SS Equipment option available with any optional V-8 engine.

ADVERTISING

Chevrolet touted the Chevelle in numerous film commercials, printed ads, and it sponsored many television series in 1960s and 1970s. *Bewitched* and *Bonanza* were two of the more-popular TV series to be sponsored by Chevrolet, and in the case of *Bewitched*, the family and friends drove a number of Chevrolet models during its run. Naturally, no Chevrolets were in the *Bonanza* series itself, but Dan Blocker (Eric "Hoss" Cartwright) was a fan of Chevrolet and was given the opportunity to own one of the first Z16-optioned Malibu SS 396s in 1965. Magazine articles and online publications have different

1969 Chevrolet Chevelle SS 396
In Detail No. 12

accounts of his ownership. One says that he rushed right out and bought one, whereas others say he was given the opportunity to own one but returned it to the dealership.

Several 60-second TV commercial advertisements touted the new 1969 SS 396. Dealer showroom brochures and other promotional materials featured taglines such as "Our Tough One," "In 10 seconds, your resistance will self-destruct," "The performance starts as soon as you're seated," "Chevelle: The concentrated Chevrolet. Just add gas," "If our competition had one like it, we'd have a lot more competition," "There's a fine line between pure sport and pure luxury. It's called Chevelle," and "Chevelles appeal to two age groups, Under 30. And over."

DEALERSHIP TRINKETS

Many dealerships had their own methods of promoting Chevelles and their dealerships. Everything from pencils and

Chevelles appealed to every age, at least as far as Chevrolet was concerned. "Chevelles appeal to two age groups. Under 30. And over." A Garnet Red SS 396 sport coupe with the black vinyl top didn't hurt either. (Photo Courtesy General Motors Media Archive)

Many dealers often had some rather unusual promotional items available at their dealership. This pot holder from Brookfield Chev. & Impl. Co. is emblazed with one of Chevrolet's taglines from 1969: "Putting You First . . . Keeps Us First."

Berger Chevrolet out of Grand Rapids, Michigan, was another high-performance Chevrolet dealer of the time. Berger Chevrolet sold a number of COPO Camaros (40) and COPO Chevelles (10) in 1969. (Photo Courtesy Berger Chevrolet)

A foam airplane with Chevrolet's tagline, "Putting You First . . . Keeps Us First" would surely keep the kiddies entertained as their parents negotiated the best deal they could from their dealer. Do you wonder how many are left today? Probably not many.

pens to yardsticks and key fobs were popular giveaways at dealers back in the day.

Most Chevrolet dealers attached either a metal dealership nameplate or decal to every Chevrolet sold. Mounting holes were often drilled into the trunk lid or tail panel to affix the dealership logos. Today, many dealers use decals or double-sided sticky lettering.

This dealership, Van Chevrolet of Mission, Kansas, holds a special place in my heart as I hung out there as a kid in the late 1960s and early 1970s. When a metal emblem was used, the dealer simply drilled holes to mount them (left on tail panel).

This Plains Chevrolet out of Amarillo, Texas, nameplate was attached to the lower left of the trunk lid of this Monaco/Hugger Orange SS 396. (Photo Courtesy Shahreyar Shafei)

Anthony Chevrolet in Fairmont, West Virginia, is still doing business selling Chevrolets. This Burnished Brown 1969 Chevelle SS 396 was sold there new more than 50 years ago. (Photo Courtesy Chris Toth)

Chevrolet touted the Chevelle's ride, which was smoother and quieter than previous years primarily due to added insulation, better weather-sealing components, and computer-generated matching front and rear springs. LeMans Blue was the second best-selling color for the 1969 Chevelle. (Photo Courtesy General Motors Media Archive)

Chevrolet dealers offered various accessories at their dealerships, such as the Chevrolet front plate, litter bags, portable spot lamps, a windshield compass, locking gas caps, pedal trim kits, etc. It isn't often that you find your Chevelle's original dealer still in business after 50 years. They change ownership, lose their dealership with GM, or simply close their doors.

Car and Driver magazine actually faulted the 1969 Chevelle for being too quiet.

"There is a very fine line between endearing mechanical excellence and an automatic, remote-control automobile," the magazine article stated. "Driving the Chevelle on any expressway is an uncomfortable hint of the future: sitting in an insulated capsule moving on a conveyer. Perfect for the four-door sedan set, but hard for the enthusiast to love . . . The Chevelle was easily the quietest car of the test. Engine noise, including intake and exhaust was almost undetectable with the windows up. Road noise and ride harshness were at a minimum."

RACING (OR LACK THEREOF)

General Motors banned racing early in 1963 when the US Justice Department was looking at General Motors sales having just over 50 percent of the entire US car market. If it increased to 60 percent, there was serious consideration to breaking up General Motors (as was done to Standard Oil). General Motors decided if it stopped putting money into factory-backed racing, it might avoid a break-up. Both Chevrolet and Pontiac had big plans for the 1963 racing season with NASCAR and the NHRA, but they never really materialized.

However, NASCAR told competitors, "We don't care if GM is supporting them or not. If it's a Chevy or Pontiac, we'll allow it in as such to compete with the other factory-backed cars."

The NHRA said, "We can't really let you run those cars (because it had a class called Super Stock, which was the best stock factory class available at the time.)"

Since you could not buy that car in the factory showroom, the NHRA created the Factory Experimental (F/X) class in which the Chevys and Pontiacs could compete.

The corporate ban on racing didn't stop General Motors from being involved with high performance though. By 1967, the Trans-Am racing series was charging full-speed ahead, and GM was developing speed parts for various teams in what was the precursor to today's GM Performance line of high-performance parts.

HIGH-PERFORMANCE DEALERS AND THE COPO CHEVELLE

Many Chevrolet dealers were involved as early as 1966 in creating their own high-performance Chevrolets apart from the factory. The General Motors ban on engines over 400 ci in its A-Body platforms (Chevrolet's Chevelle, Buick's Skylark, Oldsmobile's Cutlass, and Pontiac's Tempest) led several performance-oriented Chevrolet dealers to create their own super cars by retrofitting 427-ci engines into just about everything Chevrolet had to offer.

Dana, Berger, Baldwin, Gibb, Nickey, and of course Yenko were cashing in on the high-performance bandwagon. Camaros, Chevelles, and Novas were being outfitted with 427-ci engines and other performance goodies (such as aftermarket mag wheels, traction-bar setups, scooped hoods, special dealer striping, Hurst floor shift conversions, Sun and Stewart Warner tachometers, and more) that were available for buyers right off the dealer lots for those who ponied up the dollars.

Baldwin Chevrolet teamed up with Motion Performance to create their own brand of super car Chevelles, Camaros, and Novas. These 427 engine conversions were outfitted with as many high-performance parts and dress-up parts of the day that anyone could want and would pay for.

A rumor says that only two 1969 Phase III Chevelle SS sport coupes were ever built. The only Baldwin-Motion Phase III SS 396 that stayed with its original 396 engine is this Burnished Brown sport coupe. Outfitted with a number of factory options, it was then loaded with aftermarket goodies, such as a wood-grain steering wheel, Sun Super tachometer, Stewart-Warner gauges, a Stinger hood with hood pins, Edelbrock aluminum intake, Holley 950-cfm three-barrel carburetor, Mallory CD ignition system, and various suspension goodies to handle the beefed-up SS 396, which was backed by a modified TH400 transmission.

Chevrolet released a special Central Office Production Order (COPO) program for the Camaro in 1969 and allowed a special order to be made for an iron-block 427-ci 425-hp engine Camaro to come from the factory. Dealers saw the benefit of this because they did not have to perform the 427 engine swap at their dealerships and used the COPO program to get the 427 engines in Chevelles. An all-aluminum version of the 427 engine (designated ZL1) was available, and General Motors was able to crate up surplus

Most dealers promoted their dealerships with either decals or metal emblems with their name and location. Here, a Baldwin Chevrolet sticker is placed on the blacked-out portion of the tail panel. (Photo Courtesy Mecum Auctions)

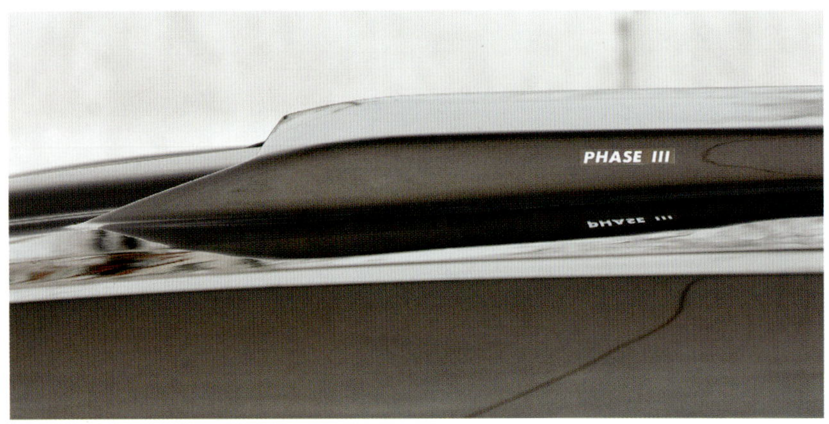

A common feature found on Baldwin-Motion Chevrolets of the era is this Corvette L88-style hood with PHASE III decal. (Photo Courtesy Mecum Auctions)

Yenko Chevrolet

Don Yenko initially ordered 50 COPO Chevelles with two subsequent orders of 25 each and ultimately wound up with a total of 99 of the estimated 350 COPO Chevelles (estimated numbers vary from 323 to 375), and Berger Chevrolet is known to have received 10 of the Chevelles. Of the 99 ordered by Yenko Chevrolet, 28 were equipped with the TH400 automatic transmission and 71 had a 4-speed manual transmission. Don Yenko's dealership in Cannonsburg, Pennsylvania, is probably the most popular COPO Chevelle supplier, but it is certainly not the only Chevrolet dealer to get into the fray.

Don Yenko's COPO Chevelles (and other Chevrolet COPO makes) were adorned with his own brand of graphics, and the 1969 Chevelle headrests were

engines and sell them directly to customers through General Motors Performance Parts, effectively creating what are known today as crate engines. The COPO program was generally reserved for municipal fleet orders, but savvy dealers used this process to circumvent the GM's 400-ci engine size limit in anything other than the Corvette and full-size Chevrolets.

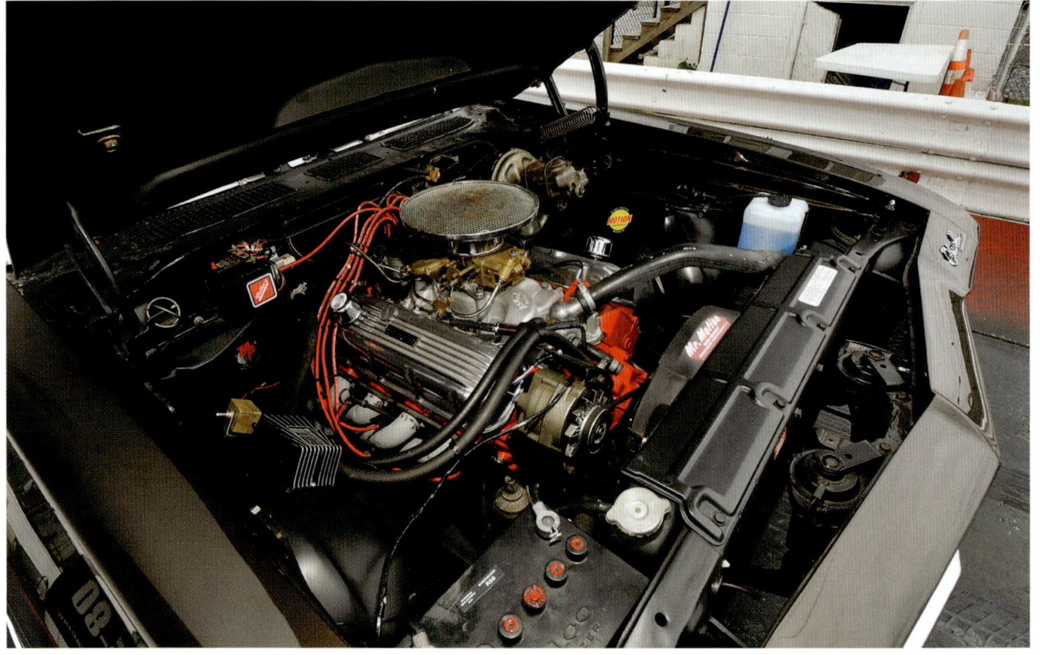

The only 1969 SS 396 Chevelle from Baldwin-Motion to retain its original 396 engine is shown. Aftermarket goodies from Mallory, Holley, and Edelbrock, and a PHASE III CD spark system, and headers are typical of Baldwin-Motion performance enhancements. (Photo Courtesy Mecum Auctions)

emblazoned with an sYc logo. There's debate over whether this meant *Yenko Sports Car* because he raced Corvairs early on or *Yenko Super Car*. The same would apply to the "Yenko/SC" on the graphics. Either way, Don Yenko is generally credited with exploiting the factory installation of the 427 engine in 1969 Chevelles via the COPO process. The special stripes were applied by his daughter and local kids at his dealership to earn extra money. Today, striping kits are sold by a number of vendors.

The 1969 COPO Chevelles were essentially converted SS 396 Chevelles with SS identification omitted in most cases. They had the Super Sport blacked-out grille but with the standard, blue Malibu bowtie emblem, the Super Sport hood, a blacked-out rear panel, 12-bolt 4.10:1 Positraction rear end, standard Malibu interior (both bench seat and bucket seat), heavy duty cooling, and chambered exhaust. Some came with a standard Malibu emblem on the steering wheel, while others had the SS emblem, and a few opted for the 3-spoke, simulated-wood steering wheel.

Don Yenko's COPO Chevelles were not only 427 ci with 425 hp, but Don's dealership added special graphics and an sYc emblem to the headrests as well. (Photo Courtesy Mecum Auctions)

Another feature unique to the Yenko COPO Chevelles was the stripe graphics. These were often applied by his daughter and local kids to earn extra money. (Photo Courtesy Rick Nelson)

Don Yenko's COPO Chevelles came with his dealership's special striping package and some additional Yenko badging. The Yenko-built COPO Chevelles were limited to the 13637-series Malibu sport coupes only, and all were equipped with the RPO L72 427-ci, 425-hp engine with square-port iron heads, a mechanical-lifter camshaft, 4-bolt main bearing caps, an aluminum high-rise intake, Holley 800-cfm carburetor, and open-element air-cleaner assembly.

Baldwin-Motion

The Baldwin-Motion COPO cars were typically outfitted with Phase III CD ignitions and fly-eye-style air cleaners and Corvette-style stinger hoods. No less than 13 COPO variations were available on the Chevelle for special equipment.

COPO Variations	
Code	Features
9562AA	4-speed manual transmission and Positraction
9562BA	TH 3-speed automatic transmission and Positraction
9562CD	Four-speed manual transmission, bucket seats, COPO tires, and special-order springs
9562CE	Same as above, excluding bucket seats
9562DD	TH 3-speed automatic transmission, bucket seats, COPO tires and special springs
9562DE	Same as above, minus bucket seats
9562EA	4-speed manual transmission, Positraction, J52 disc brakes, and L78 tires
9562FA	Same as above, except TH 3-speed automatic transmission replaced 4-speed
9566AA	Same as 9562EA with the exception of tires (used RPO PL5 14s)
9566BA	Same as 9562FA with the exception of tires (used RPO PL5 14s)
9694CA	4-speed together with 9562, 9737, and RPO J50 vacuum power brakes (This option modified RPO J52 power brakes)
9694CB	TH 3-speed automatic transmission with 9562DD, 9737LD, and RPO J50 vacuum power brakes (This option modified RPO J52 power disc brakes)
9737LD	Sports Car Conversion/Yenko. This option was 15-inch tires and rally wheels

This Baltimore COPO build sheet shows COPO options 9562DD (TH400, bucket seat, COPO tires, and special springs), 9694CB (modified J52 power disc brakes), and 9737LD Yenko Sports Car Conversion (15 inch tires and rally wheels).

1969 Chevrolet Chevelle SS 396

In Detail No. 12

RACING HERITAGE

Chevelles had their share of success in drag racing, particularly in the SS/D class where COPO versions ran. Chrysler and Ford dominated the NASCAR racing circuit, while Chevrolets were predominately being raced on quarter-mile drag strips. The 1969 Chevelles are still very popular today in drag racing. The L78 Chevelles could easily run in the high 12-second bracket at 108 mph with a bit of tuning.

PAINT

The 1967-model-year Camaro was tagged as the *hugger* from Chevrolet to promote the Camaro's road-hugging ability. Marketing being what it was, a new color for the 1969 Camaro (orange) was given the sales name *Hugger Orange*, while the same color on the Corvette was *Monaco Orange* because most Corvette colors were named for racetracks or locations. The 1969 Chevelle got in on the orange craze by offering it on the SS Equipment–optioned Chevelles only. The same marketing ploy was used with Daytona Yellow, which was both a Camaro color and a Corvette color that was an SS Equipment–optioned Chevelle color.

These two colors (Hugger/Monaco Orange and Daytona Yellow) were exclusive SS Equipment–optioned Chevelle colors and are noted on the Fisher Body number plate with either paint code 72 for Hugger/Monaco Orange or 76 for Daytona Yellow. These two colors could have

The 1969 Chevelles are still popular today in drag racing. Returned to its racing days, this L78 Chevelle has front tow bar hooks, 7-inch "cheater slicks" on steel wheels, and period-correct Cragar SS mags on the front. (Photo Courtesy Sam Griffith)

This rear view of the L78 shows old school ladder traction bars, lightweight glasspack mufflers, and 7-inch cheater slicks on steel wheels. (Photo Courtesy Sam Griffith)

Chevelle owners might not be aware of the origins of the "Hugger" term used for their 1969 SS 396 Chevelle's orange paint color. The term was coined by GM for the hugger abilities of the then-new 1967 Camaro. Hugger Orange as a paint color sales name did not appear until the 1969 model year. (Photo Courtesy GM Licensing)

been ordered on non-SS Equipment Chevelles in 1969 via the F&SO office. Chevrolet documentation lists both Hugger Orange and Monaco Orange. Of the SS Equipment–optioned Chevelles sold in 1969, Hugger/Monaco Orange came on 5,194 units and Daytona Yellow at 2,841 units.

While special-order paint colors were available on Chevelles as early as 1964 and possibly earlier for other Chevrolets, these were never generally promoted to the mass market. The F&SO office needed to approve all "non-standard" paint colors for a given year. Contrary to popular opinion, these were not COPO cars like the 1969 427 Chevelles and Camaros were. Special-order paint

cars did not require the engineering or the out-of-the-ordinary production line or offsite modifications of the COPO cars. As the F&SO name implies, special paint cars were often large-order government or company cars painted in a non-standard color, such as city/county/state vehicles painted bright orange, sometimes referred to as "road commission orange" by those in the F&SO office. Savvy dealers that knew of this option might order a few cars in a special color such as "Carolina Blue," a tribute to the fans at the University of North Carolina at Chapel Hill. Any color from any manufacturer that General Motors had access to was fair game for special order paint.

Unfortunately, General Motors did not keep detailed records of special-order paint cars. However, in 1969, 3,465 are listed as "Special & Prime" in General Motors records.

END OF THE COPO ERA

The 1969 model year was the last year of the Chevrolet high-performance COPO Camaros and Chevelles. With the 400 ci ban on A-Body General Motors platforms lifted and the introduction of the 454-ci engine early in the 1970 Chevelle model year, the COPO process wasn't needed by Chevrolet dealers any longer to make street horsepower. High performance

Daytona Yellow is one of the two SS Equipment–exclusive colors for 1969. Only 2,841 SS Equipment–optioned 1969 Chevelles were painted this color, according to General Motors records. Any other 1969 Chevelle could be ordered with the color, but it would be as a special paint, and it likely would not have the paint code number 76 on the trim tag. (Photo Courtesy Russell Muller)

The 1969 sedan pickup (El Camino) moved the backup lamps from the bumper to the tailgate, while the previous year's backup lamps in the bumper were now simply reflectors.

dealers, such as Yenko and Baldwin, continued to build Camaros, Chevelles, Novas, and even Corvettes to fill their customers' desire for additional horsepower. Don Yenko's dealership built 175 COPO Novas with the Camaro Z28/Corvette 350-ci LT1 engine, while Baldwin-Motion continued with its own 454-ci Camaros and Phase III Chevelles and Corvettes.

SAFETY FEATURES

The 1969 model year saw some new innovations in safety features. Both the front fenders and the rear quarter panels now featured safety lamps on all models. The sedan pickup (El Camino) moved the backup lamps to the tailgate, and the former lamps in the bumper were simply reflectors.

The ignition switch was moved from the dash face to the steering column. Regardless of transmission or transmission shifter location (column or floor), the Chevelle had to be put into park (automatic transmission) or reverse (manual transmission) to remove the ignition key. A locking mechanism was then engaged to prevent the steering wheel from being turned and the shift lever from being moved when the key was removed.

Front door locks were moved forward to allow easier access for the driver and front passenger with less chance of being opened from the outside when the car doors were locked.

One of the new-for-1969 safety features was a locking steering column. The ignition key moved from the dash to the steering column, and when the key was removed, the column was locked and the steering wheel could not be turned. (Photo Courtesy Chris Toth)

CHAPTER 4

HARDWARE, DRIVELINE, AND INTERIOR OPTIONS

There were very few options available on an SS 396 Equipment–optioned Malibu sport coupe, convertible, 300 Deluxe coupe or sport coupe, or sedan pickup that were not available on any other Malibu or 300 Deluxe of the same bodystyle. Certainly, the three 396 engines were one item, along with a stronger transmission (in the case of the manual 3- and 4-speeds), stronger rear ends in most cases, and the two SS 396 Equipment–optioned paint colors of Hugger/Monaco Orange and Daytona Yellow. Other items standard on the SS 396 Equipment–optioned Malibu and 300 Deluxe, such as power disc brakes, were optional on all 1969 Chevelles.

GENERAL MOTORS PRODUCTION NUMBERS

Production figures listed are from GM production reports. Since the SS 396

One of two SS 396-only colors in 1969, paint code 76 (RPO 926PP) is shown with sales name of Daytona Yellow, which was also a Camaro and Corvette color. This color and paint code 72 (RPO 927QQ) and Hugger/Monaco Orange was still a $42.15 option. (Photo Courtesy Russell Muller)

Equipment option (RPO Z25) was only available when ordering a V-8 Malibu sport coupe, convertible, sedan pickup, or 300 Deluxe coupe or sport coupe, only those three Malibu bodystyles and two 300 Deluxe bodystyles and production numbers are shown in this chapter.

Series	Bodystyle	Series/Model Number	Quantity Sold
V-8 Malibu	Two-door sport coupe	13637	286,162
V-8 Malibu	Convertible	13667	8,443
V-8 Malibu	Two-door sedan pickup	13680	39,000
V-8 300	Deluxe coupe	13427	5,620
V-8 300	Deluxe sport coupe	13437	7,181
Total production of SS 396 Equipment possible Chevelles: 346,406			
Z25 Super Sport 396 options sold: 86,307			

To date, there are no known published figures from Chevrolet on any particular option in any specific bodystyle, so it is impossible to know how many SS 396 Equipment options were ordered in any one of the five possible bodystyles. While one can calculate a statistical spread of SS options versus bodystyle, any statistical calculation is not a factual representation of the true production numbers. For example, the total Malibu sport coupes make up 82.6 percent of the total Chevelles that could have been ordered with the SS 396 Equipment options. The Malibu convertible makes up 2.43 percent, the Malibu sedan pickup makes up 11.25 percent, the 300 Deluxe coupe makes up 1.62 percent, and the 300 Deluxe sport coupe makes up 2.07 percent. Statistically, the Malibu sport coupe would get 82 percent of the SS 396 and the other series/bodystyles their percentages. Are

Series/Model	Percentage	Calculated with SS 396 Equipment Option
Malibu sport coupe	82.6%	71,290
Malibu convertible	2.43%	2,097
Malibu sedan pickup	11.25%	9,710
300 Deluxe coupe	1.62%	1,398
300 Deluxe sport coupe	2.07%	1,787

the results true and accurate production figures? No. Often, low figures are cited as fact, when in truth they are not.

Using these percentages, one can calculate the following statistical spread:

Given that these numbers are statistical calculations themselves, when trying to figure in the base 396 versus the two optional 396 engines, multiple transmissions, and other options, one can see that any numbers calculated are not much more than a guess.

PLANT PRODUCTION NUMBERS

The figures reported by GM for each month should be taken with a grain of salt. It is not known just what each plant used for a cutoff time (the last car out the door on the last workday of the month, the last car scheduled for the last workday of the month, or maybe something else entirely). There are documented cases of a VIN showing up with a Fisher Body date of a different month than the VIN sequence shows in this table. Chevelles could be built at Fisher Body and held in the "body bank" before being released for final assembly, causing a VIN sequence higher than a given production month. A Chevelle could be pulled for repairs and not released for a given time and have the same result—a later VIN sequence. Also shown in these tables is the total production reported for each plant and that plant's production percentage of all 1969 Chevelles. For example, the Leeds assembly plant at Kansas City reportedly built 181,164 1969 Chevelles, accounting for 34.66 percent of all 1969 Chevelles reportedly built, and had the highest production of 1969 Chevelles among all six assembly plants. The Oshawa, Ontario, plant had the lowest production of 34,765 1969 Chevelles, which was only 6.65 percent of the total. Since several plants missed the last month (August 1969) of production, their outputs are not a true measure of the capability of those plants.

Month	Atlanta-A	Baltimore-B*	Framingham-G
September	300001-302597	300001-308846	300001-304912
October	302598-306613	308847-318059	304913-311621
November	306614-310620	318060-326003	311622-317607
December	310621-313846	326004-333025	317608-322570
January	313847-322002	333026-344660	322571-329012
February	322003-329430	344661-355330	329013-333080
March	329431-337539	355331-367113	333081-338712
April	337540-344438	367114-378593	338713-348045
May	no production reported	378594-381442	348046-352264
June	no production reported	381443-396474	352265-360909
July	344439-346616	396475-413729	330910-367942
August	346617-356386	413730-414385	no production reported
Totals	56,386	114,385	67,942
Percentages	10.79%	21.88%	13.00%

Month	Fremont-Z*	Kansas City-K	Oshawa-1
September	300001-304595	300001-316556	no production reported (1)
October	304596-311759	316557-339096	no production reported (1)
November	311760-319029	339097-358979	no production reported (1)
December	319030-323994	358980-374064	no production reported (1)
January	323995-330138	374065-393881	300001-305317
February	330139-335464	393882-409027	305318-310442
March	335465-341235	409028-425254	310443-315261
April	341236-347446	425255-439077	315262-320566
May	347447-353627	439078-442908	320567-327938
June	353628-360184	442909-461711	327939-334650
July	360185-368119	461712-480619	335651-334765
August	no production reported	480620-481164	no production reported
Totals	68,119	181,164	34,765
Percentages	13.03%	34.66%	6.65%

*Figures are from reported GM numbers years ago, but I have found several July/August 1968 and August 1969 dated Fisher Body number plates.

(1) Early in the 1969 production year, Oshawa-built Chevelles with the SS 396 Equipment option retained the Malibu emblem script on the rear quarter panels. This convertible is documented by Vintage Vehicle Services with a delivery date of September 18, 1968. (Photo Courtesy Dustin Herbison)

Although no production figures for the Oshawa plant were available until January 1969, there were 1969 Chevelles built at the Oshawa plant in the 1968 calendar year. Another interesting fact is how the Oshawa plant began VIN sequencing with 100001 early on and did not conform to the 300001 numbering schema until later. At least 11,323 Oshawa-built 1969 Chevelles were built with the VIN sequence beginning with 100001; VIN sequence 111323 is the highest found in research so far with a production date of December 20, 1968, and shipping date of December 28, 1968.

The Oshawa, Ontario, plant (as it had done in years past) "exported" 1969 Chevelles for US sales and "imported" Chevelles from the United States. Typically, the Chevelles imported into Canada were bodystyles not built at Oshawa, such as the Greenbrier and Concours Estate station wagon series and sedan pickups. However, documentation from Vintage Vehicle Services shows that other Chevelles, such as the 13637 V-8 Malibu sport coupe, were also exported to the United States and 10,828 Malibu sport coupes were exported, while only 9,612 were built for sale in Canada. Of those built for sale in Canada, 903 were SS 396 Equipment optioned.

There are some discrepancies between production figures for Chevelles imported from Canada and the figures released by General Motors in the above matrices and Vintage Vehicle Services documentation. These differences are minor, but it is worthy to note here.

Model/ Series	GM Production Figure	Vintage Vehicle Services Figure
13427	361	358
13437	388	386

While Vintage Vehicle Services in Canada does an excellent job of helping one document a true SS 396 built in or sold in Canada, the numbers often do not add up. For example, on one report, the 13637 Malibu sport coupe produced for sale in Canada shows that 9,612 were built (903 with Z25 and 294 of those optioned with the L34 engine), but another report shows the same Malibu sport coupe built for Canada with 427 having the L35. So, of the 903 Z25-optioned Malibu sport coupes built for sale in Canada (294 with the L34 and 427 with the L35), the sum is only 721. That figure is 182 units short of the 903 Z25-optioned cars sold because no L78 engines were sold in Chevelles built in Canada for the Canadian market. All L78-optioned 1969 Chevelles were imported from the United States for Canadian dealers.

There is no way to know how many of any particular series/bodystyle that an individual US plant may have produced, much less how many Z25 SS 396 Equipment options were processed by a given plant. What is known is that Atlanta did not build any convertibles in 1969, only three plants (Baltimore, Fremont, and Kansas City) built sedan pickups, and the Oshawa plant did not build any RPO L78-optioned Chevelles. There will always be claims of someone's Chevelle being "1-of-some number" and very "rare" or "special" based on conjecture, poor math skills, or maybe just an aggressive sales technique.

VEHICLE IDENTIFICATION NUMBERS

The 1969 Chevelle VIN format is identical to the 1965–1968 model years with the exception of a few bodystyle number changes and plant designations. The VIN is an alphanumeric 13-character set. This is an example: 136379K345678. Like previous years, each plant had its own method of stamping the VIN on the VIN plate. The breakdown is as follows:

1	Chevrolet Division of General Motors (GM)
34	Series designation (V-8 300 Deluxe)
36	Series designation (V-8 Malibu)
27	Bodystyle/model (300 Deluxe coupe)
37	Bodystyle/model (300 Deluxe/Malibu two-door sport coupe)
67	Bodystyle/model (V-8 Malibu convertible)
80	Bodystyle/model (V-8 Malibu sedan pickup)
9	Model year
K	Final assembly plant (here it is the Kansas City plant)
345678	Sequential production number for this 1969 Chevelle at the Kansas City plant.

These are the five US assembly plants for 1969 and their GM designation letter:

A	Atlanta, Georgia
B	Baltimore, Maryland
G	Framingham, Massachusetts
F	Fremont, California
K	Kansas City, Missouri

The Oshawa, Ontario, plant VIN format was essentially the same with the difference being the plant designation. Instead of a letter in the seventh character position, the number *1* is used, such as 1363791345678 (except the early-model-year VIN sequencing explained earlier).

Sequence Number

The six-digit sequence number is the sequential production number for that plant assigned to that Chevelle. Each 1969 assembly plant began with sequence number 300001. Sequence numbers were not assigned by series or bodystyle but rather as each car was scheduled to be assembled. Chevelles of the same series or bodystyle were fairly random, meaning that a V-8 Malibu two-door sport coupe could be sequence number 301000 and followed by a 6-cylinder 300 Deluxe sport coupe with sequence number 301001. While it is certainly possible to find two 1969 Chevelles of the same series and bodystyle with the same sequence numbers, the assembly plants were unique. Production at the Baltimore plant exceeded 100,000 units in early July, and the Kansas City plant exceeded 100,000 units in mid-February 1969, causing the sequence number to roll over to 400,000.

VIN Plate Location

The VIN plate itself stayed at the top front driver's side of the dash, where it could be read from outside the car looking through the windshield. It was attached to the dash via a special plate with the same rosette-head rivets as before.

Identifying a GM of Canada SS 396 Chevelle is pretty straight forward. GM of Canada coded some options on its Fisher Body number plates, such as *L35* here, indicating the 396-ci 325-hp engine. (Photo Courtesy SS 396 Registry)

No RPO Z25 Coding on Chevelles

Since RPO Z25 was an option just like any other option (such as a radio, air conditioning, vinyl top, etc.), there is nothing in any US or Oshawa plant's VIN to indicate that the SS 396 Equipment option was ordered.

There is nothing on any US-built Fisher Body number plate, trim tag, or cowl tag that proves a 300 Deluxe coupe or sport coupe, a Malibu sport coupe, convertible, or sedan pickup was ordered with the SS 396 Equipment option. There is speculation that the Kansas City and Baltimore Fisher Body number plates may indeed show if the SS 396 Equipment option was part of a Chevelle order by using the letter *L* on the trim tag. To date, no official documentation has turned up to prove that this letter *L* from either plant indicates the SS 396 Equipment option, but there is certainly overwhelming circumstantial evidence for the argument. On the other hand, Oshawa coded certain options on its trim tags, using either the L35 or L34 engine option code. The L78 was not available as an option on a Canadian-built Chevelle, so one will never find the L78 engine code on an Oshawa trim tag. All L78-optioned Chevelles sold by a Canadian dealer were imported from the United States.

ENGINE CODES

The Flint and Tonawanda engine plants used unique two-letter engine suffix codes for Chevelles to designate the engine displacement (cubic inch size), horsepower ratings, and transmission type (manual or automatic). This mattered primarily because a manual-transmission car required a pilot bushing in the crankshaft, and an automatic-transmission car required a flexplate. Very late in the model year, the engine plants began using a three-letter engine suffix code, and a few found their way into late 1969 Chevelles. The displacement rose from 396 to 402 ci in these Turbo-Jet engines.

For consistency the 402 L35, L34, and L78 SS 396 Equipment–option engine will be referred to as a "396" because GM still referenced them as a 396 or 400-4.

Code	HP-RPO	Transmission	Notes
JA	325-L35	Manual	A.I.R.
JC	350-L34	Manual	A.I.R.
JD	375-L78	Manual	A.I.R.
JE	350-L34	TH400	A.I.R.
JK	325-L35	TH400	C.C.S.
JV	325-L35	Manual	A.I.R./H.D. clutch
KB	350-L34	Manual	A.I.R./H.D. clutch
KD	375-L78	Manual	A.I.R./H.D. clutch
KF	375-L78	TH400	A.I.R.
KG	375-L78/ L89	Manual	A.I.R./L89 aluminum head option
KH	375-L78/ L89	TH400	A.I.R./L89 aluminum head option
KI	375-L78/ L89	Manual	A.I.R./H.D. clutch/ L89 aluminum head option

Late-model-year 3-letter engine suffix codes are the same as the 2-letter codes listed above with the addition of the letter C at the beginning, such as CJA, CJC, etc. However, not all late-model-year Mark IV engines with a 3-letter engine suffix code are 402 ci. There are documented true late-model-year 396-ci Mark IV engines with a 3-letter suffix code.

Most 1969 396 engines were equipped with the Air Injection Reactor (A.I.R.) system regardless of transmission type. The exception is the 325-hp L35 engine with the TH400 3-speed automatic transmission because this combination used the Controlled Combustion System (C.C.S.) to meet emission standards.

Tonawanda 396/402 Engine Production

RPO	HP	Transmission	Suffix	Production	Notes	
L35	325	Manual	JA	32,999	396-ci displacement	Total L35 engines: 60,684
L35	325	Manual	CJA	1,528	402-ci displacement	Total L35 cars: 59,786
L35	325	TH400	JK	24,771	396-ci displacement	Total L35 service engines: 898
L35	325	TH400	CJK	1,386	402-ci displacement	

RPO	HP	Transmission	Suffix	Production	Notes	
L34	350	Manual	JC	12,454	396-ci displacement	Total L34 engines: 17,937
L34	350	Manual	CJC	370	402-ci displacement	Total L34 cars: 17,358
L34	350	TH400	JE	5,034	396-ci displacement	Total L34 service engines: 579
L34	350	TH400	CJE	79	402-ci displacement	

RPO	HP	Transmission	Suffix	Production	Notes	
L78	375	Manual	JD	7,356	396-ci displacement	Total L78 engines: 8,876
L78	375	Manual	CJD	33	402-ci displacement	Total L78 cars: 9,486
L78	375	TH400	KF	1,471	396-ci displacement	More L78 cars than engines: 610
L78	375	TH400	CKF	16	402-ci displacement	

RPO	HP	Transmission	Suffix	Production	Notes	
L78/L89	375	Manual	KG	333	396-ci displacement	Total L78/879 engines: 412
L78/L89	375	Manual	CKG	12	402-ci displacement	Total L78/89 cars: 400
L78/L89	375	TH400	KH	66	396-ci displacement	Total L78/L89 service engines: 12
L78/L89	375	TH400	CKH	1	402-ci displacement	

RPO	HP	Transmission	Suffix	Production	Notes	
L72	425	Manual	MQ	277	427-ci displacement (COPO)	Total 427 engines (COPO): 373
L72	425	TH400	MP	96	427-ci displacement (COPO)	Total 427 Chevelles (COPO): 323
						Total 427 service engines (COPO): 50

The L89 aluminum head production figures should be added to the L78 total. As a result, the difference is only 210 more cars than engines as listed in the L78 section.

Engine Production Date and Usage Identifier

A total of 448,501 8-cylinder-engine Chevelles were built or imported into the US. One can calculate the number of each 8-cylinder engine by using the number of each optional engine sold (with

those not accounted for being the base 307-ci engine). For example, it is known from sales-figure reports that 9,486 L78 engines were ordered (including those with the L89 aluminum head option); 17,358 L34 engines were ordered (leaving 59,786 L35 engines based on Z25 SS 396 Equipment–option sales); 23,315 LM1 engines were ordered; 30,099 L48 engines were ordered; and 53,969 L65 engines were ordered, which leaves 254,811 with the base 307 engine.

The Tonawanda engine assembly plant built all 396-, 402-, and 427-ci displacement engines. This engine will have the letter *T* followed by the same 4-digit date code and the engine identification code. An example of a Tonawanda engine plant stamp might read *T1025JA*, where *T* is for Tonawanda, *10* is for October, *25* is the 25th of October, and *JA* is the suffix code for an L35 with manual transmission.

General Motors standardized the stamping of all engines with what is commonly called a "partial VIN," "CON VIN," or "VIN derivative" on either the engine pad or rough cast area by the oil filter pad, identifying the model year, plant,

This Fremont, California, engine pad stamp shows the Tonawanda engine plant identifier (*T*), the engine's assembly date (*0124*), the engine/transmission identifier (*JE* for the L34 and TH400), and the partial VIN of the Chevelle in which the engine was installed. (Photo Courtesy SS 396 Registry)

and last six digits of the sequence number in which the engine was installed in 1968. Final-assembly plants pretty much standardized on these stamps with uniform clarity, utilizing what is referred to as a "gang stamp," where all the characters are put in a handheld apparatus and all characters are stamped at the same time, giving the stamp a uniform appearance. An associated partial VIN should also be stamped on the firewall behind the heater box and on top of the frame rail on the driver's side just aft of the rear end. However, these two hidden locations were not always stamped.

It is interesting to note that the 396-/402-ci displacement engines built at the Tonawanda engine plant appear to have their date and ID stamped before the heads were installed and stamped on the left-most portion of the pad, leaving the right-most portion available for the partial VIN at the assembly plant.

Batteries

The 1969 Chevelle engines had three different batteries. The 6-cylinder and

Both the Atlanta, Georgia, and Kansas City, Missouri, final assembly plants stamped the Chevelle's partial VIN on the rough cast area by the oil filter. All other Chevelle plants stamped the Chevelle's partial VIN on the engine pad along with the Tonawanda engine plant's date/code stamp. (Photo Courtesy SS 396 Registry)

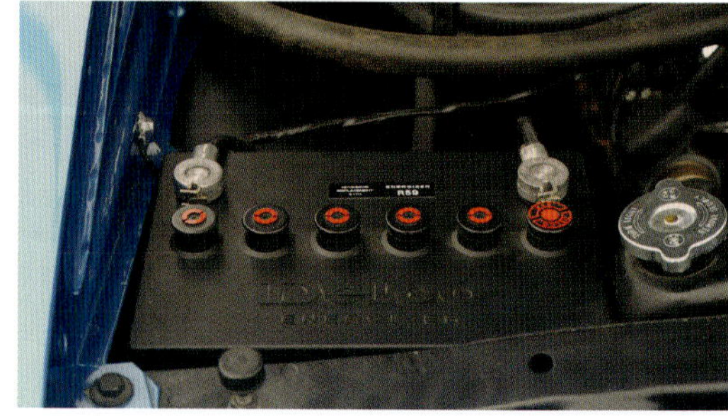

The Delco R59 energizer was the standard battery for the 350-ci and 396-ci engines in 1969 and can now be replicated with a battery topper for as little as $60 as opposed to a period-correct battery at $360.

base 307 V-8 battery, number 1980032 (Y55), is a 12-volt 45-amp/hour unit with 54 plates. This top-post battery has the positive terminal on the passenger's side of the battery. The 350 V-8 and the 396 V-8 battery, number 1980030 (R59), is a 12-volt 61-amp/hour unit with 66 plates and has the positive terminal on the driver's side of the battery. The heavy-duty battery option (RPO T60–R69) is a 12-volt 70-amp/hour unit with 66 plates. The heavy-duty battery was optional in any 1969 Chevelle.

WHEELS AND TIRES

The SS 396 Equipment option included (for the first time) a special wheel exclusive to the SS 396. These SS 396 wheels were not available as an option on any non-SS 396 Chevelle, and no other wheel was optional on the SS 396 Chevelle.

Tires for all coupes, sport coupes, and convertibles were blackwall F70-14 two-ply (four-ply rating bias belted) with either raised white letters, the optional red stripe, or the white stripe at no cost.

The El Camino came with a larger G70-14 tire, although early El Camino dealer information (dated November 8, 1968) says F70-14 tires.

Original equipment tires for all SS 396 coupes, sport coupes, and convertibles were RPO PL5, a two-ply, four-ply rating nylon tire in F70-14 size. The SS 396 El Camino was RPO PK4 in G70-14 size and red stripe. Various optional fiberglass belted tires in raised white letter and red or white stripes were available.

Goodyear, Firestone, and Uniroyal are known suppliers of tires for the 1969 Chevelle SS 396. There is no known breakdown of which manufacturer's tire was the most popular by percentage.

F70-14 bias-belted red-stripe tires were optional on the SS 396 coupe, sport coupe, and convertible at no cost. The fiberglass-belted version of the tire was optional. The same tire as a bias-belt or optional fiberglass-belt was available on the sedan pickup in a G70-14 size. (Photo Courtesy Chris Toth)

The first year that a special wheel was exclusive to any SS 396 Equipment–optioned Chevelle was 1969. Neither hubcaps or wheel covers were available with an SS 396, and the 14x7-inch SS 396 wheels were not an option on any non-SS 396 Chevelle. (Photo Courtesy L78 Registry)

Yenko COPO Chevelles with the COPO option 9737LD Yenko Sport Car Conversion received 15x7 rally wheels and F70-15 Wide Tread GT tires. It is possible that if this tire/wheel combination was not available at the time, a 14x7 rally wheel and F70-14 tire was used. (Photo Courtesy Rick Nelson)

Typically, the buyer received whichever manufacturer's tire the factory installed that day, but most dealers swapped tires (and wheels) to the customer's preference when asked (assuming the same size and stripe/letter sidewall markings). In all instances, the fiberglass-belted tire was optional over the standard two-ply (four-ply rating) bias-belted tire. Tire availability and cost is based on April 1, 1969 changes.

Several F70-14 and G70-14 tires were available as options on non-SS 396 Equipment–optioned Chevelle coupes, sport coupes, convertibles, and sedan pickups.

Coupe, Sport Coupe, and Convertible Tires		
Size/Material	RPO	MSRP
F70-14/two-ply (four-ply rating) Original Equipment White-Lettered Blackwall	PL5	N.C.
F70-14/two-ply (four-ply rating) Original Equipment Red Stripe	PW8	N.C.
F70-14/two-ply (four-ply rating) Original Equipment White Stripe	PW7	N.C.
F70-14/B Fiberglass Belt Red Stripe	PY5	$26.25
F70-14/B Fiberglass Belt White Stripe	PY4	$26.25
F70-14/B Fiberglass Belt White Lettered Blackwall	PL4	$26.25
El Camino Tires		
Size/Material	RPO	MSRP
G70-14/two-ply (four-ply rating) Red Stripe	PK4	N/A*
G70-14/two-ply (four-ply rating) Original Equipment White Stripe	PX9	N.C.
G70-14/B Fiberglass Belt Red Stripe	PY7	$25.95
G70-14/B Fiberglass Belt White Stripe	PX8	$25.95

*The RPO PK4 tire has been found on at least one Fremont, California, build sheet for a sedan pickup with the SS 396 option and a June 1969 build date. GM's Accumulative Production report shows that 4,436 buyers opted for this tire, but to date, no cost associated with the tire has been found.

Coupe, Sport Coupe, and Convertible Tires		
Size/Material	RPO	MSRP
Replaces (5) 7.35-14/two-ply (four-ply rating) Original Equipment Blackwall		
F70-14/two-ply (four-ply rating) Original Equipment Red Stripe	PW8	$72.30 (1)
F70-14/two-ply (four-ply rating) Original Equipment White Stripe	PW7	$72.30 (1)
F70-14/B Fiberglass Belt Red Stripe	PY5	$98.35 (1)
F70-14/B Fiberglass Belt White Stripe	PY4	$98.35 (1)
F70-14/two-ply (four-ply rating) Original Equipment White-Lettered Blackwall	PL5	$72.15 (1)

El Camino Tires		
Tire Size/Material	RPO	MSRP
Replaces (5) 7.7.5-14/two-ply (four-ply rating) Original Equipment Blackwall (Models 13480 and 13680 with RPO N10 Dual Exhausts and Bench Seat)		
F70-14/two-ply (four-ply rating) Original Equipment Red Stripe	PW8	$58.50
F70-14/two-ply (four-ply rating) Original Equipment White Stripe	PW7	$58.50
F70-14/two-ply (four-ply rating) Original Equipment White-Lettered Blackwall	PY5	$84.85

Coupe, Sport Coupe, and Convertible Tires		
F70-14/B Fiberglass Belt White Stripe	PY4	$84.85
F70-14/two-ply (four-ply rating) Original Equipment White-Lettered Blackwall	PL5	$58.20

(1) GM's Truck Data Book (for the sedan pickup) has different pricing for these options than the coupe, sport coupe, and convertible pricing. The manufacturer's suggested retail prices (MSRPs) shown are taken from the Chevelle price list. The El Camino price list shows:

RPO	MSRP
PW8	$73.45
PW7	$73.45
PY5	$99.80
PY4	$99.80
PL5	$73.15

TRANSMISSIONS

The base (or standard) transmission for the SS 396 was a heavy-duty, full-synchromesh, floor-shifted 3-speed manual transmission, RPO MC1. The MC1 heavy-duty manual 3-speed transmission was also an option on both 350-ci engines as well. Manual 4-speed transmissions and the TH400 3-speed automatic transmission were optional with any SS 396 Chevelle.

Manual Transmissions

The three 396 engines came standard with a heavy-duty, floor-shifted 3-speed manual transmission. All other V-8 engines came with a column-shifted, 3-speed manual transmission. Those ordering the 350-hp L34 and 375-hp RPO L78 engine could opt for the Muncie close-ratio M21 or the M20 wide-ratio Muncie. Chevrolet's Power Team chart does not show the L35 325-hp engine as available with the M21, although it certainly could have been ordered. Sales reports show that 13,786 RPO M21 and just 1,276 RPO M22 transmissions were sold in 1969 Chevelles. The RPO M20 manual 4-speed transmission could be either the aluminum Muncie unit or one of the two cast-iron Saginaw

A Muncie heavy-duty, full-synchromesh, floor-shifted manual 3-speed transmission was the base transmission with the SS 396 Equipment option. It is shown here with optional full-vinyl bench seat. (Photo Courtesy Rocco Regina)

units used with engines that had less than 300 hp. All fell under the RPO M20 option code, and the particular engine with which an M20 was ordered dictated which particular transmission was used. A 307-ci engine ordered with an M20 would get a 2.85:1 low-gear Saginaw, the 350-2 RPO L65 350-ci engine ordered with an M20 would get a 2.54:1 low-gear Saginaw, and the 350-4 RPO L48 350-ci engine and both the L35 and L34 396-ci engines with an M20 would get the 2.52:1 low-gear aluminum-case Muncie 4-speed transmission.

Automatic Transmissions

An SS 396 buyer could also opt for the TH400 automatic transmission. The TH400 was column shifted unless a Malibu sport coupe, convertible, or sedan pickup customer ordered bucket seats and a console, and it was always column shifted when it was ordered with the 300 Deluxe coupe or sport coupe because the bucket seats (and therefore console) were not available as options in the 300 Deluxe series. When those two options (bucket seats and console) were ordered, the shifter was moved to the floor in the center console. The console option is what dictated the TH400 transmission having the horseshoe or staple floor-shift assembly; bucket seats without a console was still column-shifted. While the TH400 was sold under one RPO M40 code, there were variations in the internal pieces for strength, and the engine ordered determined exactly which TH400 was installed.

Several TH400 transmissions were used in 1969 Chevelles depending on the engine's advertised horsepower, and again, this was determined by the engine. The specific TH400 can be identified by a metal tag riveted to the case with a two-letter code identifying the transmission.

The L35 325-hp 396 engine has the letters *CC*, and the L34 350-hp 396 engine has the letters *CE*. The TH400 transmission for the RPO L78 engine and the RPO L72 427 COPO engine have the letters *CX*.

Other information found on the TH400 transmission tag includes the Julian date on which the transmission was built along with the serial number of the transmission itself. The build date begins with the number *1* for the calendar year of the transmission (beginning on January 1, 1968, in the case of all 1969 TH400 transmissions) and continuing sequentially until the last transmission for that model year was built. So, it is not uncommon to see

The TH400 transmission for a 1969 SS 396 Chevelle can be identified by the metal tag attached to the transmission's case. The CE code is for a 396-ci 350-hp engine. (Photo Courtesy SS 396 Registry)

a Julian date in the 400–500 range. For example, a Julian date of *413* means the 413th day since January 1, 1968, which is February 17, 1969.

Although the RPO M35 2-speed Powerglide transmission was still available, the TH350 3-speed automatic transmission (RPO M38) was new for 1969 and optional behind both 6-cylinder engines as well as the 307-ci displacement and 350-ci displacement 8-cylinder engines. Chevrolet's Accumulative Production Report indicates that 135,503 M38 TH350 transmissions and 226,784 2-speed Powerglide transmissions sold. Neither the M35 or the M38 were available behind any 396 engine.

REAR-AXLE IDENTIFICATION, CODES, AND RATIOS

The 1969 12-bolt rear end carried a casting number of 3917124 or 3959038, and the 10-bolt unit was number 3917123. As a general rule of thumb, the 10-bolt unit was used behind all engines with an advertised horsepower rating of less than 300, whereas a 300-plus-hp rating received the 12-bolt unit.

A ratio identification code and the date and plant of assembly should be stamped into the front of the passenger-side axle tube. GM calls for this stamp to be 8 to 10 inches inboard of the brake's backing plate, but it has been found almost anywhere on the passenger-side front. Not a great deal of care was taken to stamp this information. Often, it is not too deep, so it can be hard to find, and it requires a good scraping of the road grime from this area to see it.

This stamping is in the format of a 2-letter prefix code for the ratio information, and generally, a 4-digit number indicates the month and day of assembly. For example, a typical 12-bolt 3.31:1 ratio from the Buffalo, New York, assembly plant might be *CW 1025 B.*

The casting date of the center section is found in one of the webs of the center section and will have a letter code for the month, a 1- or 2-digit number for the date of that month, and a 1-digit year code. An example might be *C219* for March 21, 1969, or *F 2 9* for June 2, 1969. Month letters are *A* through *L* for January through December. Typically, the same ratio was not offered in both the 10-bolt and 12-bolt rear ends. For example, the 3.07:1 ratio is a 12-bolt ratio, whereas the 3.08:1 ratio is a 10-bolt ratio. The 2.73:1, 3.31:1, and 3.55:1 are exceptions for 1969 and available in both 10-bolt and 12-bolt rear ends. Where applicable, it is noted what that particular ratio came behind by matching a particular ratio to a known build sheet or other documentation.

Available Gear Ratios	
Type	**Ratios**
10-bolt	2.56:1, 2.73:1, 3.08:1, 3.36:1, 3.55:1
12-bolt	2.73:1, 3.07:1, 3.31:1, 3.55:1, 4.10:1, 4.56:1, 4.88:1
Four rear-axle assembly plants supplied rear ends to Chevelle assembly plants.	

Code	Assembly Plant Location
B	Buffalo, New York
G	Chevrolet Gear & Axle (Detroit, Michigan)
W	Warren, Michigan
K	McKinnon Industries (St. Catharines, Ontario)

Engine	Transmission	Without Air-Conditioning				With Air-Conditioning			
		Std	Econ	Perf	Spec	Std	Econ	Perf	Spec
L35	3-speed	3.31:1	3.07:1	3.55:1	3.73:1 or 4.10:1	3.31:1	3.07:1	–	–
	M20	3.55:1	3.31:1	3.73:1	3.07:1 or 4.10:1	3.31:1	3.07:1	–	–
	TH400	3.31:1	3.07:1	–	2.73:1	3.31:1	3.07:1	–	–
L34	3-speed M20	3.55:1	3.31:1	3.73:1	4.10:1	3.31:1	3.07:1	–	–
	M21	3.55:1	3.31:1	3.73:1	4.10:1	3.31:1	–	–	–
	TH400	3.55:1	3.31:1	3.73:1	3.07:1 or 4.10:1	3.31:1	3.07:1	–	–
L78	3-speed M20	3.55:1	3.31:1	3.73:1	3.07:1 or 4.10:1	N/A	N/A	N/A	N/A
	M21/ M22 TH400	3.55:1	3.31:1	3.73:1	4.10:1	N/A	N/A	N/A	N/A

All ratios are available with Positraction; 3.73:1 and 4.10:1 were only available with Positraction.

Axle Ratios with or without AC

General Motors has standard rear-axle gear ratios depending on the engine, transmission, and whether or not air-conditioning was ordered, unless an optional gear ratio was ordered by the customer.

Frame braces were used on all SS 396 Equipment–optioned 1969 Chevelles just as they had been in 1967 and 1968 SS 396-series Chevelles to provide structural reinforcement to the frame.

INTERIOR TRIM CODES

The Malibu-series sport coupe, convertible, and sedan pickup could be ordered with the optional A51 bucket seats, regardless of whether the SS 396 Equipment option was ordered or not. The 300 Deluxe series coupe and sport coupe could not be ordered with A51 bucket seats regardless of whether the SS 396 Equipment option was ordered

First used for the 1967 Chevelle model year, frame braces (shown here with natural finish) were used to strengthen the frame. The braces reinforced the frame rails to the rear cross member. (Photo Courtesy Rick Nelson)

Ordering bucket seats did not require ordering a console. The SS 396, when equipped with either the standard heavy-duty manual 3-speed or one of the optional manual 4-speed transmissions, was always floor shifted. When no console was ordered, the gear shift knob was black. (Photo Courtesy Chuck Frame)

or not, and only black cloth/vinyl or vinyl, medium blue cloth/vinyl, or medium green cloth/vinyl were available in the 300 Deluxe. The sedan pickup only offered a selection of three colors when it came to bucket seats: 756 for black, 765 for dark blue, and 771 for saddle. Otherwise, one could opt for a black, dark blue, or saddle-colored all-vinyl bench seat.

Bucket seats were not standard, not even with the SS 396 Equipment option. Bucket seats were always an option. *Coated fabric* continued to be Chevrolet's way of saying vinyl. True leather seating was never a Chevelle option. The coated fabric designation is synonymous with

When an optional manual 4-speed transmission was ordered along with bucket seats, the gear shift knob was chrome. A bench-seat Chevelle with a 4-speed transmission gear-shift lever received a black plastic gear-shift ball with white shift pattern.

numbers, while a 4-speed manual transmission with a console received a chrome gear-shift ball.

A change for the 1969 model year seat locks for bucket seats was the positioning of the release. The seat release for the 1967 and 1968 model years was located on the outside of the seat. For the 1969 model year, it was moved to the center of each bucket seat, while the bench seat release remained in essentially the same location as previous years (on the lower left and lower right of the driver's and passenger's sides).

COPO-optioned Malibu interiors were no different than standard Malibu sport coupe interiors. Although, some COPO Chevelles came with an SS steering wheel or the optional N34 wood-grain plastic steering wheel, most were equipped with a standard Malibu steering wheel with the blue bowtie emblem in the center of the crossbar.

The TH400 was a column-shift assembly (even with bucket seats) unless a

A change for the 1969 model year was the location of the seat back lock/release mechanism. This made it easier for a passenger in the back seat to unlock the bucket seat back for easy exit and lessened the chance of anything snagging on the release from the 1967 and 1968 style.

vinyl as it is used in this book. The A51 bucket seat option did not require the D55 center console. Of the 79,871 1969 Chevelles ordered with bucket seats, 72,201 buyers opted for the console as well. Manual transmissions were always floor shifted in an SS 396, whether it was the standard heavy-duty 3-speed or one of the optional manual 4-speed transmissions. The gear-shift ball on a non-console car is black with a white shift pattern and

As with any Malibu ordered with bucket seats and no console, the manual 4-speed shift lever received a black gear shift ball with white lettering/pattern, even on a COPO Chevelle. Note the Malibu steering wheel, period-correct Stewart Warner tachometer, and lack of SS 396 emblems. (Photo Courtesy Rick Nelson)

console was ordered. In that case, the shifter mechanism was moved to the console.

Cloth and vinyl bench seats were standard in all Chevelle sport coupes. Convertibles and sedan pickups automatically received coated fabric (vinyl) seats. An all-vinyl bench seat covering was optional in the sport coupe for $12.65.

Seat Coding and Materials

Bench Seat Code	Color/Material	Possible SS 396 Equipment Series/Style
751	Black Ransom Cloth, Coated Fabric	13427-13437
752	Black Pattern Coated Fabric	13427-13437
760	Med. Blue Ransom Cloth, Coated Fabric	13427-13437
786	Med. Green Ransom Cloth, Coated Fabric	13427-13437
753	Black Rior Cloth, Coated Fabric	13637
755	Black Coated Fabric	13637-13667-13680
762	Dark Blue Rior Cloth	13637
764	Med. Blue Coated Fabric	13667-13680
770	Antique Med. Saddle Coated Fabric	13680
779	Med. Turquoise Rior Cloth, Coated Fabric	13637
782	Midnight Green Rior Cloth, Aff. Midnight Green Coated Fabric	13637
783	Med. Green Rior Cloth, Coated Fabric	13637
784	Med. Green Coated Fabric	13637
787	Med. Red Coated Fabric	13637-13667
790	Aff. Parchment Coated Fabric	13637-13667
795	Aff. Midnight Green Coated Fabric	13637

Bucket Seat Code	Color/Material	Possible SS 396 Equipment Series/Style
756	Black Coated Fabric	13637-13667-13680
765	Metallic Dk. Blue Coated Fabric	13637-13667-13680
771	Antique Med. Saddle Coated Fabric	13680
785	Metallic Med. Green Coated Fabric	13637
788	Med. Red Coated Fabric	13637-13667
791	Aff. Parchment Coated Fabric (black carpet)	13637-13667
796	Metallic Dk. Green Coated Fabric	13637

BOB CRANSTENS CHEVROLET
MT WHITNEY & HAZEL
RIVERDALE CALIF

Car Shipper
Dealer Copy
06-114

I.D. No.

CHEVROLET

Dealer Order No.
OQM656

FREMONT, CALIF.

2,673 00

8 MALIBU SPT COUPE

152 00

2,825 00

Code	Description	Price	
915	65-65 OLYMPIC GOLD		
784	GREEN VINYL TRIM	12	65
A01	SOFT-RAY TINTED GLASS	36	90
A82	HEAD RESTRAINTS	16	90
C60	4-SEASON AIR CONDITIONING	376	00
J50	POWER BRAKES	42	15
L48	300-HP TURBO-FIRE 350 V8	68	50
M40	TURBO HYDRA-MATIC	200	65
N40	POWER STEERING	105	35
P01	FULL WHEEL COVERS	21	10
P62	7.75 X 14 WHITEWALL TIRES	33	45
U35	ELECTRIC CLOCK	15	80
U63	AM PUSHBUTTON RADIO	61	10
U80	REAR SEAT SPEAKER	13	20

THIS CAR INCLUDES ALL THESE FEATURES—
ASTRO VENTILATION, HIDE-A-WAY WIPERS,
GLOVE COMPARTMENT LIGHT, CARPETING,
FRONT SEAT BACK LATCHES, FRONT SHOULDER
BELTS, LIGHTER, BODY SIDE STRIPING,
LUGGAGE COMPARTMENT MAT.

Car Shipper paperwork for a Fremont, California, Malibu sport coupe shows RPO A82 Head Restraints, costing $16.90. When this option was removed on January 1, 1969, the cost was simply absorbed into the Chevelle's base price with a $17 increase.

Credit Dept. OK		Date Pur.				Zone	Car Shipper No.	Date of Execution	Invoice Numb
Dealer Code	Car No. or Route	Date Shipped		LOS ANGELES, CAL		06		11/12/68	L05370
06 114	TRUCK	11/11/68		Financial Location					

Type / Dir. Ord. No.	Serial Number / Options and Extra Equip.	Description	Suggested Retail Price	Car & Option Price	D & H	Amount	Key Number
13680		8 CUSTOM EL CAMINO	2706.00	2003.94	207.00	2210.94	
	06A01FA	SOFT-RAY TINTED GLAS	37.70	26.60	2.70	29.30	
	06A82ZB	HEAD RESTRAINTS	17.25	12.16	1.25	13.41	
	06B37MA	FLOOT MATS 2 FRONT &	6.50	4.56	.50	5.06	
	06C60RC	4-SEASON AIR CONDITI	384.15	271.32	27.15	298.47	
	06M40NC	TURBO HYDRA-MATIC TR	226.80	168.00	16.80	184.80	
	06N40EL	POWER STEERING	107.60	76.00	7.60	83.60	
	06PX8AB	E70 X 14 WHITE STRIP	25.95	19.00	.95	19.95	
	06T6CEA	HEAVY-DUTY BATTERY	16.15	11.40	1.15	12.55	
	06U14CJ	SPECIAL INSTRUMENTAT	96.85	68.40	6.85	75.25	
	06U63AC	AM PUSHBUTTON RADIO	62.45	44.08	4.45	48.53	
	06ZJ9CC	AUXILIARY LIGHTING	14.00	9.88	1.00	10.88	
	06Z25AB	SS 396 EQUIPMENT	370.15	261.44	26.15	287.59	
	C677CCD	MED SADDLE VINYL TRI	.00	.00	.00	.00	

** CONTINUED ON NEXT INVOICE FORM **

Dealer invoice paperwork for a Fremont, California, sedan pickup shows RPO A82 Head Restraints costing $17.25. When this option was removed on January 1, 1969, the cost was simply absorbed into the Chevelle's base price with a $17 increase.

The 300 Deluxe coupe and sport coupe could not be ordered with bucket seats, even when the SS 396 Equipment option was ordered.

Headrests for both bench- and bucket-seat Chevelles were included in overall pricing, but there was an option to delete the headrests (RPO AR1) prior to December 31, 1968, and 774 buyers opted to do just that. On January 1, 1969, this delete option was no longer available. RPO A82 was used for the headrest on paperwork prior to the December 31, 1968, cutoff, and there was even a cost associated with the option. The cost of RPO A82 ranged from $16.90 to $17.25.

When the SS 396 Equipment option was ordered, the steering wheel (and steering column) was always black, regardless of the interior color, with a raised *SS* on the center bar. Door panels on the Malibu sport coupe, convertible, and sedan pickup received an *SS 396* emblem that replaced the standard *Malibu* emblem. The SS 396 Equipment–optioned 300 Deluxe coupe and sport coupe did not get this *SS 396* emblem, and the standard *Chevelle* emblem remained. The bright trim above the glove

All SS 396 Equipment–optioned Chevelles came standard with a black steering column and black steering wheel with an SS emblem centered on the horizontal bar. Note also the lack of gauges. Gauges were always an option, even on SS 396 Equipment–optioned Chevelles. This particular SS 396 is optioned with the RPO U35 clock, however. (Photo Courtesy Chris Toth)

1969 Chevrolet Chevelle SS 396
In Detail No. 12

When the Z25 SS 396 Equipment option was ordered on a Malibu sport coupe, convertible, or sedan pickup, one of the interior changes was the *SS 396* emblem on the door panel replaced the *Malibu* emblem. The SS 396 Equipment–optioned 300 Deluxe did not get an emblem change on its door panels. (Photo Courtesy Russell Muller)

box also announced *SS 396* on the Malibu series and 300 Deluxe series. Aside from these changes, the Malibu-series interior remained untouched.

EXTERIOR PAINT CODES

The 1969 Chevelles were available in 17 solid colors. Any 1969 Chevelle could have been ordered in 15 of these. Only

One piece of interior trim with the SS 396 Equipment option is the bright trim above the glove box with an *SS 396* nameplate in place of Malibu. The 300 Deluxe series did not have a nameplate over the glove box area unless it was SS 396 Equipment optioned. (Photo Courtesy Chris Toth)

One of two SS 396-only colors in 1969. Paint code 72 (RPO 927QQ) is shown with sales name of both *Hugger Orange* and *Monaco Orange* in GM documentation. Whatever color you choose to call it, this color and paint code 76 (RPO 926PP) Daytona Yellow was still a $42.15 option. (Photo Courtesy Rocco Regina)

paint code 72 (Hugger/Monaco Orange) and paint code 76 (Daytona Yellow) were reserved for SS 396 Equipment–optioned Chevelles. However, at least one 1969 COPO Chevelle from Kansas City has been found with paint code 72. Chevrolet's production reports indicate that only 5,194 SS 396 Equipment–optioned Chevelles were ordered with Hugger/Monaco Orange and 2,841 with Daytona Yellow.

There is no breakdown of how many of any of the five series/bodystyles any color was ordered with or how many were convertibles or ordered with vinyl tops

This is a Frost Green (or Frost Lime) SS 396 Equipment–optioned Malibu sport coupe with a dark green vinyl top. The car is riding on modern BFGoodrich T/A radials. Frost Green was the most popular color as far as sales go in 1969: 81,883 Chevelles were painted in this color. (Photo Courtesy Jeff Steffes)

1969 Chevrolet Chevelle SS 396
In Detail No. 12

with these two colors. Even on an SS 396 Equipment–optioned 1969 Chevelle, these two colors were a $42.15 option.

Chevrolet changed the way that color choices were depicted on documentation. Where 1965–1968 used a letter for the paint code and a number for a convertible or vinyl top, 1969 changed to a two-digit number for the lower and upper body color and a letter for a convertible or vinyl top. For example, where a 1968 Tuxedo Black car would have paint code of *A-A*, the same Chevelle in 1969 would show a paint code of *10-10*. A 1968 Tuxedo Black convertible with a white convertible top was coded *A-1*, while the same Chevelle in 1969 showed *10-A*.

The following list shows the paint codes for 1969 Chevelles and the sales name. Along with the solid colors, six two-tone combinations were available on any bodystyle except the convertible, station wagon, and sedan pickups.

Paint Code (RPO)	Sales Name/Color
10 (910AA)	Tuxedo Black/black
40 (916YY)	Butternut Yellow/yellow
50 (911CC)	Dover White/white
51 (923EE)	Dusk Blue/dark blue
52 (913RR)	Garnet Red/red
53 (922DD)	Glacier Blue/blue
55 (921KK)	Azure Turquoise/turquoise
57 (920VV)	Fathom Green/dark green
59 (919WW)	Frost Green*/lime
61 (918SS)	Burnished Brown/dark brown
63 (917MM)	Champagne/champagne
65 (915GG)	Olympic Gold/gold
67 (914NN)	Burgundy/maroon
69 (912BB)	Cortez Silver/silver
71 (924FF)	LeMans Blue/bright blue
72 (927QQ)	Hugger/Monaco Orange/orange
76 (926PP)	Daytona Yellow/bright yellow
Two-Tone Paint Code (RPO)	**Sales Names/Colors**
53/50 (954DC)	Glacier Blue/Dover White
53/51 (955DE)	Glacier Blue/Dusk Blue
51/53 (956ED)	Dusk Blue/Glacier Blue
65/50 (957GC)	Olympic Gold/Dover White
55/50 (958KC)	Azure Turquoise/Dover White
61/63 (959SM)	Burnished Brown/Champagne

*Also referred to as Frost Lime in some General Motors documentation.

Several special-order paint colors have been found with 1969 Chevelles. DuPont code 926-96881, often referred to as *Carolina Blue*, continued to be a favorite, especially in the Southeastern US. (Photo Courtesy Streetside Classics)

Top Codes and Colors

Convertible and vinyl top codes changed from a number to a letter beginning with the 1969 model year. There was no charge for the optional black convertible top. Either white or black could be ordered with any lower body color.

Convertible Top Code	Color
A	White (standard RPO C05AA)
B	Black (optional RPO C05BB)

A vinyl top was optional on the 300 Deluxe coupe and sport coupe, the Malibu sport coupe and El Camino, and four-door sedans and four-door sport sedans. Costs varied depending on the particular body-style, and even some price increases occurred during the model year. The vinyl top color choice had no effect on pricing.

Vinyl Top Code	Color
B	Black (RPO C08BB)
C	Dark Blue (RPO C08CC)
E	Parchment (RPO C08EE)
F	Dark Brown (RPO C08FF)
G or S	Midnight Green (RPO C08GG)

Color by Percentage

This table lists the single-tone colors used, number reported, and the percentage of the color's use. With the exception of paint codes 72 and 76 for Hugger/Monaco Orange or Daytona Yellow respectively, which are SS 396 colors, the number of a color is for all Chevelles.

Paint Code (RPO)	Sales Name	Sold	Percent (2)	Percent (3)
10 (910AA)	Tuxedo Black	7,441	1.48	1.55
40 (916YY)	Butternut Yellow	27,028	5.37	5.61
50 (911CC)	Dover White	33,152	6.59	6.88
51 (923EE)	Dusk Blue	19,230	3.82	3.99
52 (913RR)	Garnet Red	29,449	5.85	6.11
53 (922DD)	Glacier Blue	36,377	7.23	7.55
55 (921KK)	Azure Turquoise	22,980	4.57	4.77
57 (920VV)	Fathom Green	41,226	8.19	8.56
59 (919WW)	Frost Green	81,883	16.27	17.00
61 (918SS)	Burnished Brown	17,724	3.52	3.68
63 (917MM)	Champagne	23,610	4.69	4.90
65 (951GG)	Olympic Gold	44,118	8.77	9.16
67 (914NN)	Burgundy	14,415	2.86	2.99
69 (912BB)	Cortez Silver	20,419	4.06	4.24
71 (924FF)	LeMans Blue	51,060	10.14	10.60
72 (927QQ)	Hugger Orange	5,194	1.03	1.08
76 (926PP)	Daytona Yellow	2,841	0.56	0.59
–	Special/Prime	3,465	0.69	0.72
–	Total	481,612	–	–

There are several caveats here:

- It is assumed that convertibles and Chevelles with vinyl tops are included in these numbers because the colors of two-tone cars were kept separately.

(2) The percentages represent all 1969 Chevelles.

(3) The percentages represent solid colors only.

(4) The percentages represent two-tone combinations only.

This table lists two-tone colors used, the number reported, and the percentage of the usage.

Paint Codes (RPO)	Sales Names	Sold	Percentage (4)
954DC	Glacier Blue/Dover White	4,590	21.16
955DE	Glacier Blue/Dusk Blue	798	3.68
956ED	Dusk Blue/Glacier Blue	833	3.84
957GC	Olympic Gold/Dover White	5,057	23.31
958KC	Azure Turquoise/Dover White	4,754	21.92
959SM	Burnished Brown/Champagne	5,658	26.09

Discrepancies have been found with 1969 Chevelle production numbers versus other General Motors production numbers. For example, the total number of 1969 Chevelles by series/engine type is 503,352 (including those imported from Canada), yet paint color sales numbers only add up to 503,302, which is 50 Chevelles fewer. According to the last reported VINs by each plant, the total is either 487,996 (excluding Oshawa) or 522,761 (including Oshawa). General Motors reported no production at Oshawa until January 1, 1969. However, it is known that 1969 Chevelles were being built at the Oshawa plant as early as September 1968 and had VIN sequences beginning with 100,001. VIN sequencing at Oshawa did not start using 300,001 until January 1. The point is that published production figures (even those using GM's own documentation) must be taken with a grain of salt.

EXTERIOR/INTERIOR COLOR COMBINATIONS

Some interior trim colors (and their associated trim codes) were limited to specific paint colors and recommended by Chevrolet. Optionally, a buyer could override the recommended color, but the orders had to be verified by the dealer. However, specific trim styles were limited to certain series and could not be overridden. For example, one could not order a Malibu-series interior trim in a Chevelle 300 Deluxe series.

Malibu 13680 Series Interior Colors and Codes

Trim	Black	Dark Blue	Saddle
Vinyl Bench	755	764	770
Vinyl Bucket	756	765	771

Malibu 13680 Exterior/Interior Colors

Exterior Color	Black	Dark Blue	Saddle
10 – Tuxedo Black	X	X	X
40 – Butternut Yellow	X	–	X
50 – Dover White	X	X	X
51 – Dusk Blue	X	X	–
52 – Garnet Red	X	–	–
53 – Glacier Blue	X	X	–
55 – Azure Turquoise	X	–	–
57 – Fathom Green	X	–	X
59 – Frost Green	X	–	–
61 – Burnished Brown	X	–	X
63 – Champagne	X	–	X
65 – Olympic Gold	X	–	X
67 – Burgundy Maroon	X	–	X
69 – Cortez Silver	X	X	–
71 – LeMans Blue	X	–	–
72 – Orange*	X	–	–
76 – Yellow*	X	–	–

Malibu 13637-13667 Series Interior Colors and Codes

Models		Trim	Black	Dark Blue	Med Green	Dark Green	Med Turq	Med Red	Parch Black
37	67								
X		Cloth	753	762	783	782	779	–	–
	X	Vinyl	–	764	–	–	–	–	–
X		Vinyl	–	–	784	795	–	–	–
X	X	Vinyl	755	–	–	–	–	787	790
X	X	Bucket	756	765	–	–	–	–	–
X		Bucket	–	–	785	796	–	–	–

Exterior Color	Black	Dark Blue	Med Green	Dark Green	Med Turq	Med Red	Parch/Black
10 – Tuxedo Black	X	X	X	X	X	X	X
40 – Butternut Yellow	X	–	–	–	–	–	X
50 – Dover White	X	X	X	X	X	X	X
51 – Dusk Blue	X	X	–	–	–	–	X
52 – Garnet Red	X	–	–	–	–	X	X
53 – Glacier Blue	X	X	–	–	–	–	X
55 – Azure Turquoise	X	–	–	–	X	–	X
57 – Fathom Green	X	–	X	X	–	–	X
59 – Frost Green	X	–	X	X	–	–	X
61 – Burnished Brown	X	–	–	–	–	–	X
63 – Champagne	X	–	–	–	–	–	X
65 – Olympic Gold	X	–	–	–	–	–	X
67 – Burgundy Maroon	X	–	–	–	–	X	X
69 – Cortez Silver	X	X	–	X	X	X	X
71 – LeMans Blue	X	X	–	–	–	–	X
72 – Orange*	X	–	–	–	–	–	X
76 – Yellow*	X	–	–	–	–	–	X
Two-Tone Lower/Upper							
Glacier Blue/ Dover White	X	–	–	–	–	–	X
Glacier Blue/Dusk Blue	X	–	–	–	–	–	X
Dusk Blue/Glacier Blue	X	–	–	–	–	–	X
Olympic Gold/Dover White	X	–	–	X	–	–	X
Burnished Brown/Champagne	X	–	–	–	–	–	X
Azure Turquoise/Dover White	X	–	–	–	X	–	X

Vinyl Roof Colors	
B	Black (all exterior colors)
E	Parchment (all exterior colors)
C	Dark Blue (Dover White, Cortez Silver, Glacier Blue, and Dusk Blue)
F	Dark Brown (Olympic Gold, Butternut Yellow, Champagne, and Burnished Brown)
S or G	Midnight Green (Tuxedo Black, Dover White, Frost Green, and Fathom Green)

*In the above matrices from GM's documentation, orange and yellow are referenced generically and not by their sales names of Hugger or Monaco Orange and Daytona Yellow.

Folding top color: Choice of white (standard) or black (optional) with all exterior colors

A customer could have requested any interior color with any exterior color. However, if the choice did not coincide with the approved color combinations listed here, the dealer had to note on the order form that the color choice was accurate. Interior colors were limited by the series though. For example, the Nomad and 300 Deluxe series were still limited to interior colors available in those series and bodystyles.

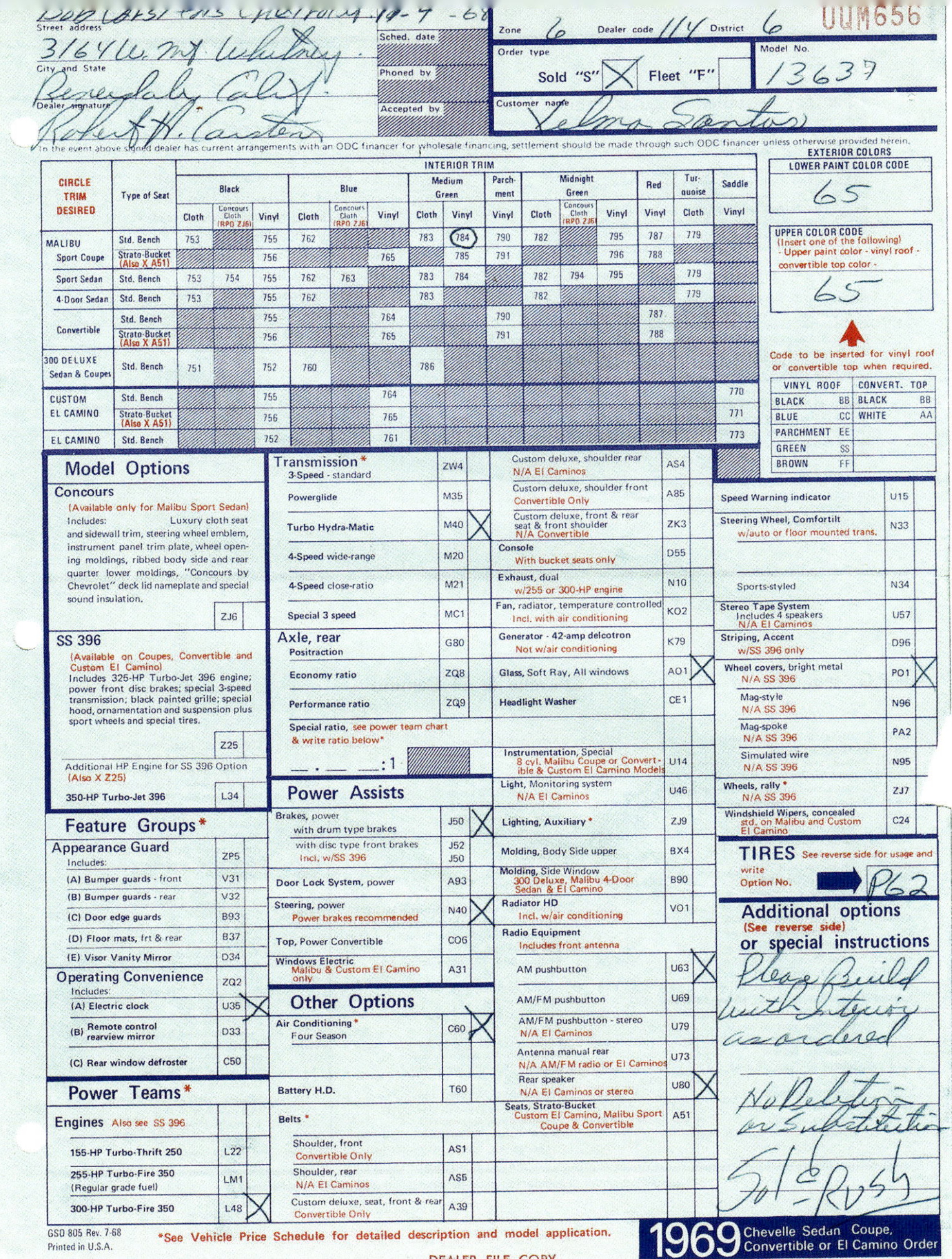

This is a dealer order form requesting paint code 65 (Olympic Gold) with interior code 784 (Medium Green vinyl bench seat). Since this combination was not an approved/suggested color combination, the dealer had to note the special request with the addition of "No deletion or substitution."

SPORT STRIPING COLORS (RPO D96)

The standard color for RPO D96 and Malibu Side Accent stripes was dependent on the top color (if it was a vinyl or convertible top) and in some cases on the interior color. The RPO D96 stripes were an option only when the SS 396 Equipment option was ordered.

Exterior	SS 396 All except convertible	Convertible		Vinyl Roof				
		Black Top	White Top	Black	Parchment	Dark Brown	Dark Blue	Midnight Green
–	–							
Tuxedo Black	White (a)	White	White	White	White	–	–	White
Dover White	Black (b)(c)	Black	Black	Black	Black	–	Black	Black
Glacier Blue	Black	Black	White	Black	White	–	Black	–
Dusk Blue	White	White	White	White	White	–	White	–
LeMans Blue	White	Black	White	Black	White	–	–	–
Olympic Gold	Black	Black	White	Black	White	Black	–	–
Burnished Brown	White	White	White	White	White	White	–	–
Azure Turquoise	Black	Black	White	White	Black	–	–	–
Frost Green	Black	Black	White	Black	White	–	–	Black
Burgundy	Red	Red	White	Red	White	–	–	–
Cortez Silver	Black (c)	Black	White	Black	White	–	Black	–
Garnet Red	Black	Black	White	Black	White	–	–	–
Champagne	Black	Black	White	Black	White	Black	–	–
Fathom Green	White	White	White	White	White	–	–	White
Butternut Yellow	Black	Black	Black	Black	Black	Black	–	–
Monaco Orange	White	Black	White	Black	White	–	–	–
Daytona Yellow	Black	Black	Black	Black	Black	–	–	–
(a) Red with Black or Red interior (b) Bright Blue with Blue interior (c) Red with Red interior								

FISHER BODY NUMBER PLATES

A Fisher Body number plate (also known as a trim tag, cowl tag, firewall tag, etc.) is a plate affixed by Fisher Body to assist dealers with body, interior, and exterior paint attributes of the car. For the purpose of uniformity, they are referred to here as a trim tag. They were not necessarily used by workers at the Fisher Body side of the assembly plant because those workers already had paperwork showing the style, interior seat type and material, and exterior paint colors.

Each assembly plant had its own standard operating procedures regarding which pieces of data went on its trim tag. Three US plants (Atlanta, Fremont, and Framingham) had trim tags that measured 1-3/4-inch x 4-inch. Baltimore and Kansas City continued using the 1-3/4-inch x 4-inch through at least 12A and 11A, respectively, before changing to the more-square 2-3/16-inch x 3-1/2-inch plate. Oshawa trim tags measure 2-3/16-inch x 3-1/2-inch. Regardless of the final assembly plant, all *blank* trim tags had certain text already stamped on them. The assembly plant supplied the body date, trim code, paint code information, and any specific information that the particular plant deemed necessary.

The Kansas City assembly plant is suspected of using the letter *L* under the lower body color to indicate the SS 396 conversion for the body trim. It is quite possible that the letter *L* on a Baltimore trim tag may represent the same thing.

The letter *L* has been found on Baltimore trim tags for every possible SS 396 Equipment–optioned model to date and has not been found on any series/model that could not be SS 396 Equipment optioned (a station wagon or four-door sedan/sport coupe). However, like Kansas City, tangible proof has not yet surfaced of its meaning.

None of the Atlanta, Framingham, or Fremont trim tags have single or multiple letters that might indicate an SS 396 Equipment–optioned Chevelle. One 99.99-percent correct method of identifying an SS 396 Equipment–optioned Chevelle is if the trim tag has either paint code 72 or paint code 76 because these two colors were only an option when the SS 396 Equipment option was ordered.

WARRANTY CARD (PROTECT-O-PLATE)

Although using the Fisher Body trim tag to identify an SS 396 Equipment–optioned 1969 Chevelle is possible, it is a sketchy way at best based on the final assembly plant. Aside from finding either a build sheet or body/chassis broadcast copy sheet, each new Chevrolet owner was supplied with a warranty book, and in that book was a metal plate with information on the car. This information included the car's VIN, carburetor type, engine-stamped date and two-letter suffix code, the rear-end identification code and date, the transmission code and date, and some basic options. Since the 396 engine, the Turbo Hydra-matic transmission, and/or Muncie 4-speed transmission were SS

The warranty card Protect-O-Plate for 1969 Chevelles has the car's VIN, carburetor type, engine date and suffix code, rear-axle gear ratio code and date, month of assembly, transmission-type code and date, and several options (as noted by the *1* and *3* numbers). (Photo Courtesy Shawn McCourry)

396-only, a valid engine and/or transmission code on the warranty card indicates that the SS 396 Equipment option was ordered with the Chevelle. In this example, the engine code on line 2, (T0319JD) indicates an L78 engine with a manual transmission built on March 19. Line 3 identifies a Muncie 4-speed transmission (P9B25) built on February 25. The plate itself is reverse stamped but mirrored here so that it's easily readable.

Naturally, take proper precautions when considering a purchase based solely on the warranty card. These are fairly easy to reproduce: blanks and the machines with which they were stamped (an addressograph) are readily available today.

REGULAR PRODUCTION OPTIONS BY APPLICABILITY

The only options available with the SS 396 Equipment models are listed here. A few of these options were part of RPO Z25 and are noted with an asterisk. Not listed are options that would not be available on an SS 396 Equipment–optioned

A $21.10 option on the Chevelle 300 Deluxe series two-door coupe, RPO B90 Door Widow Frame Molding bright trim, dressed up the 300 Deluxe–series Chevelle coupe. Note that the coupe retained the vent wing; sport coupes and convertibles did not.

Chevelle due to the series and/or bodystyle, and some options were available for Chevelles not optioned with RPO Z25.

The 13427-series Chevelle 300 Deluxe coupe is often referred to as a *two-door post* (pillared) *coupe*, or *two-door sedan* because of the B-pillar between the front door glass and rear quarter glass—as opposed to the 300 Deluxe and Malibu sport coupe, or the hardtop without the B-pillar. Chevrolet changed the designation of the *two-door sedan* to *coupe* in 1968 with the bodystyle designation change from *11* to *27*.

While many options were very popular, such as the push-button radio and air-conditioning, some were not so common, such as the RPO D33 remote driver's mirror (20,025 reported ordered), RPO A31 electric windows (4,583 reported ordered), RPO N34 wood-grain plastic steering wheel (7,515 reported ordered), RPO U46 lamp monitoring (2,041 reported ordered), RPO V75 traction compound and dispenser (278 reported ordered), U26 under-hood lamp (34,114 reported ordered), or C50 rear window defogger (15,372 reported ordered). Since most of these options were available on any 1969 Chevelle, optioning an SS 396 Equipment Chevelle with one of these makes them even more desirable today.

Auxiliary Light Group

The RPO U26 under-hood lamp could be ordered as a stand-alone option or could be part of the Auxiliary Light Group (RPO ZJ9) that included various lamp items depending on the bodystyle. This group included (A) ashtray light, (B) courtesy light, (C) glove compartment

The driver-side outside mirror for 1969 changed from the earlier year's round style to a 5-inch rectangular style. A passenger-side mirror was offered as a dealer installed accessory but not a factory option. (Photo Courtesy Chris Toth)

1969 Chevrolet Chevelle SS 396
In Detail No. 12

RPO D33 L.H. Remote Mirror was ordered on 20,025 (only about 4 percent) of the 1969 Chevelles for the princely cost of $10.55. The D33 L.H. Remote Mirror was part of the Operating Convenience Group RPO ZQ2, but strangely, it was not included in the option when the SS 396 was ordered, according to the Features and Specifications Manual. (Photo Courtesy Chris Toth)

RPO V75 Traction Compound Dispenser is a truly rare option with only 278 reportedly sold in 1969. The idea was to use a switch under the dash to spray the compound on the rear tires to aid traction under slippery conditions. (Photo Courtesy Chris Toth)

RPO U46 Light Monitoring System had been an option since the 1967 model year in Chevelles. It was available on all 1969 Chevelles except the sedan pickup. This system monitored the left and right turn signals and headlamp beam with fiber optics. The front lamps and optics were installed on the final assembly line. (Photo Courtesy Chris Toth)

light, (D) luggage compartment light, (E) under-hood light, and (F) mirror map light. The particular bodystyle dictated which lights were included in the ZJ9 option.

Model	Options
Convertible	includes A, D, E, and F
Malibu sedan and sport coupe	includes A, B, D, E, and F
300 Deluxe models	includes A, B, C, D, E, and F
Sedan pickup models	includes A, B, E, and F

Since the glove compartment lamp was standard with the Malibu, it is not included in the Auxiliary Light Group. A convertible has the courtesy light (or dome light) omitted in favor of the standard under-dash courtesy lamp, so that lamp in not included in the group.

Remote Mirror

The remote driver-side mirror is another interesting item. Depending on the series, and even other options ordered, the RPO ZQ2 Operating Con-

Available as RPO U26 Underhood Lamp, the placement of the lamp varies depending on the engine type; Chevelles equipped with a 6-cylinder or 396 engine have the lamp on the passenger's side of the hood, whereas other V-8s are on the driver's side of the hood. (Photo Courtesy Russell Muller)

The tachometer, oil pressure, water temperature, and battery amp gauges were an option on with any V-8 engine 300 Deluxe coupe and sport coupe as well as the Malibu sport coupe, convertible, and sedan pickup under RPO U14. The only difference in any gauge option was the redline of the tachometer based on the particular engine size. The 1969 model year was the last year that an oil pressure gauge was included in the option in a Chevelle. (Photo Courtesy Russell Muller)

venience Group option included the following items: (A) Electric Clock, (B) L. H. Outside Remote Control Mirror, and/or (C) Rear Window Defogger.

Model	Options
All models except Malibu sport coupe or convertible	includes A, B, and C

Model (Malibu sport coupe or convertible)	Options
Without special instrumentation or SS 396	includes A, B, and C
With special instrumentation without SS 396	includes B and C
With SS 396 without special instrumentation	includes A and C
With SS 396 and special instrumentation	includes C

There does not seem to be data on the ZQ2 group option for the El Camino. One can infer that the same options were included with the exception of the rear window defogger because this option was not available with the El Camino anyway. Additionally, there are not any figures for the number of ZQ2 options sold as a group.

It is interesting to note that according to one source, the L. H. Outside Remote Control Mirror was not included in the ZQ2 Operating Convenience Group

RPO U15 is the Speed Warning Indicator option available on any 1969 Chevelle. The driver sets the maximum desired speed (white needle), and if the speedometer reaches that speed, a warning buzzer alarms the driver. Only 4,372 buyers opted for this. The 1969 model year was the last year for this option in a Chevelle.

when the SS 396 Equipment option was ordered. However, another GM source (the 1969 Chevrolet Passenger Car Prices book) does not exclude the L. H. Outside Remote Control Mirror in this group. It's odd that a non-SS 396 Equipment–optioned Malibu sport coupe or convertible would have it included but not an SS 396 Malibu sport coupe or convertible. Possibly, this was a running change during the model year. The electric clock was not included in the group when special instrumentation (U14 gauges) was ordered because the clock was already a part of the special instrumentation option.

Chevrolet's own documentation has a contradiction here. In its "Options and Accessories When Installed by Chevrolet" table, the SS 396 is not mentioned as an exclusion—only the Malibu. But in the "Chevelle 1969 Feature & Specification Manual," the SS 396 is specifically mentioned and specifically notes the L. H. Outside Remote-Control Mirror is not available when the Operating Convenience Group is ordered along with the SS 396 option.

A right-hand mirror was available as an accessory for Chevelles in 1969 under part number 993595 but was never a regular production option. The mirror is identical in size and appearance to the left-hand standard production mirror. The outside mirrors changed shape from previous years and were now a 5-inch rectangular mirror that replaced the previous 4-inch round mirror.

RPO F41 Special Suspension

Contrary to popular belief, RPO F41 special suspension was not part of the SS 396 Equipment option and did not come standard. The option was relatively unknown in 1969, resulting in the very low sales reported by General Motors at 722 units. This option included a special front stabilizer with special duty bushings, rear-axle lower control arm reinforcements, a rear stabilizer bar, and special front and rear springs with matching shock absorbers (a $29.50 option in 1969 or just over $200 today). It is understandable why such an expensive option saw low sales.

It wasn't necessarily an option, but when a Malibu-series El Camino (135/13680) was ordered with bucket seats, the spare tire behind the passenger's seat received a cover. This cover was furnished by Fisher Body and installed in the car by the final assembly-line worker.

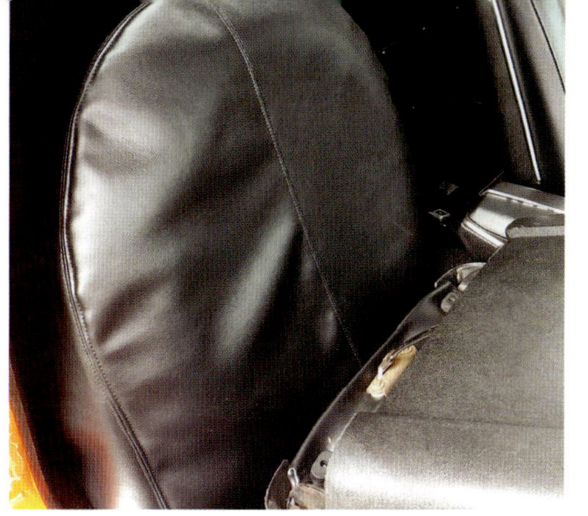

When any Custom El Camino (13580 or 13680 style) was ordered, Fisher Body supplied a spare tire cover, and this cover was installed on the final assembly line. (Photo Courtesy Bill Rose)

SS 396 Engines/Exhaust

The RPO Z25 SS 396 option included the base L35 engine with the RPO L34 396/350 engine, which added $121.15 to the cost, and the RPO L78 being a $252.80 option. An aluminum head option, RPO L89 added a whopping additional $647.75 to the RPO L78's cost and could only be ordered with the L78 engine. Although the horsepower rating was the same at 375 with or without the L89 heads, the lighter weight of the heads reduced the front-end weight. The L89 aluminum heads shaved about 70 pounds from the front-end weight, and 400 buyers checked the L89 box on the order form. The L35 and L34 engines

The 396-ci 325-hp engine was the base powerplant for the SS 396 Equipment option. This engine featured a single-snorkel air-cleaner assembly with a flash chromed lid. Rocker-arm covers and the oil filler cap on the passenger-side rocker arm cover are also flash chromed as part of the standard SS 396 engine dress-up. The A.I.R. was standard for the 396-ci 325-hp engine with a manual transmission.

The optional RPO L34 396-ci 350-hp engine differed visually from the 325-hp L35 engine with an open-element air-cleaner assembly. The L34 engine was outfitted with GM's A.I.R. emission system regardless of transmission.

The optional RPO L78 396-ci 375-hp engine utilized the same open-element air-cleaner assembly as the L34 350-hp version. However, the L78 was equipped with an aluminum high-rise intake manifold and a Holley 4-barrel carburetor as opposed to the cast-iron intake and Quadrajet 4-barrel carburetor found on the 325-hp and 350-hp engines.

could be ordered with RPO C60 air-conditioning due to their limited RPM range and hydraulic-lifter camshafts, where the optional L78 engine could not be ordered with air-conditioning due to its higher RPM range and mechanical-lifter camshaft. Both the L35 and L34 engines were outfitted with GM's venerable Quadrajet 4-barrel carburetor, while the L78 was equipped with a Holley 4-barrel carburetor (part number 3959164-GE and Holley list number 4346).

All SS 396 Chevelles came with dual exhaust. The chambered exhaust was fitted on early-production-year L34 and L78 Chevelles with no conventional mufflers. These were short lived as standard items because of numerous state and local authority complaints. The NC8 chambered exhaust remained available for all three engines as a $15.80 option, although only 4,143 buyers opted for the system.

Early production exhaust tip ends were rolled but replaced with non-rolled units when these were discovered to rust rather quickly due to moisture retention. Later exhaust extensions have a flatter surface to allow condensation to exit easily.

Only 400 of the RPO L78 engine buyers opted for the RPO L89 aluminum head option in 1969. General Motors did not increase the horsepower rating of the L89-equipped L78 engine (the rating was kept at 375 hp). A buyer had to check two boxes on the order form, one for the L78 engine at $252.80, plus an additional $647.75 for the L89 option.

Both the base L35 325-hp engine and the optional L34 350-hp engine used a Quadrajet 4-barrel carburetor. Several variations of the Quadrajet were used depending on the engine size, transmission type, and whether the engine was equipped with GM's A.I.R. or the C.C.S. emissions equipment. (Photo Courtesy Chuck Frame)

A Holley carburetor was used on the RPO L78 375-hp engine. This carburetor has its GM part number (3959164-GE) and Holley list number (*List 4346*) stamped on the air horn. An aluminum high-rise intake manifold is used on the L78, whereas the L35 and L34 have a cast-iron intake manifold.

Chambered exhaust was used on early SS 396 Equipment–optioned Chevelles with both the L34 350-hp and L78 375-hp engines. Noise complaints from local and state authorities caused General Motors to relegate the chambered exhaust system to an option under RPO NC8. (Photo Courtesy Robert Killingsworth)

Later model year SS 396 exhaust tips no longer had a rolled lip that tended to retain moisture and rust after a short period of time. The cheater slicks shown here were used in Stock class drag racing. (Photo Courtesy Sam Griffin)

Early 1969 model year SS 396 exhaust extensions (on all except the sedan pickup) featured a rolled lip. It was soon discovered that this lip retained moisture and caused rust to form.

The only 396 engine that was not equipped with GM's A.I.R. emission equipment was the L35 325-hp version when optioned with the TH400 transmission. In this instance, the engine was outfitted with GM'sC.C.S. emissions equipment. Note the heat tube from the passenger-side exhaust manifold to the air-cleaner housing snorkel.

The emissions tune-up label for both the RPO L35 and RPO L34 (as well as the 265-hp RPO L48) carried the broadcast code of *CG*. This sticker was located on the driver's side of the panel and positioned so the instructions could be read from the front of the Chevelle.

The emissions tune-up label for the RPO L78 carried the broadcast code of *CH*. This sticker was located on the driver's side of the panel and positioned so the instructions could be read from the front of the Chevelle.

Emissions Equipment

All 1969 396 engines were outfitted with GM's Air Injection Reactor (A.I.R.) system for emissions control except one particular engine/transmission combination: the base L35 with the TH400 3-speed automatic transmission.

This particular engine and transmission combination was fitted with GM's Controlled Combustion System (C.C.S.) to control emissions. The C.C.S. also required special carburetor and distributor settings and a higher engine operating temperature. The carburetor (a Rochester/Carter Quadrajet 4-barrel unit) incorporated an idle fuel-limiting mechanism to control the fuel mixture and exhaust emissions even if the idle mixture screws are turned out too far. The engine tune label for the L48 (350-4), L35, and L34 engines carry broadcast code *CG*, and the L78 carries broadcast code *CH*.

SS 396 Transmissions

The SS 396 could be ordered with one of three Muncie 4-speed transmissions or the TH400 3-speed automatic as an option over the standard heavy-duty manual 3-speed transmission. The three optional Muncie transmissions were the wide-ratio M20 with a 2.52:1 low gear, the close-ratio M21 with a 2.20:1 low gear, or the heavy-duty M22 rock crusher with a 2.20:1 low gear. The TH400 3-speed automatic came in three versions depending on the particular engine and can easily be identified by the code letters on the metal tag riveted to the transmission case: *CC* for the L35, *CE* for the L34, and *CX* for the L78.

Beginning in 1969, the Muncie stamped information format changed, and the Muncie date identification stamp can be used to identify an M20, M21, or M22 case by the use of the letter *A* for the M20 version, *B* for the M21 version, or *C* for the M22 version. This letter follows the month/day build date, although some very early (August/September) 1968 transmissions built for the 1969 model year have been reported that did not include this identifying letter. For example, *P911A* would identify a Muncie (P) built in November (9) of 1968, the eleventh day (11), and identifies as an M20 (A). The month letter date codes are A-January, B-February, C-March, D-April, E-May, H-June, K-July, M-August, P-September, R-October, S-November, and T-December. Transmissions dated September through December were actually built in the 1968 calendar year but are identified as 1969 transmissions, as noted in the first 9 in the stamp.

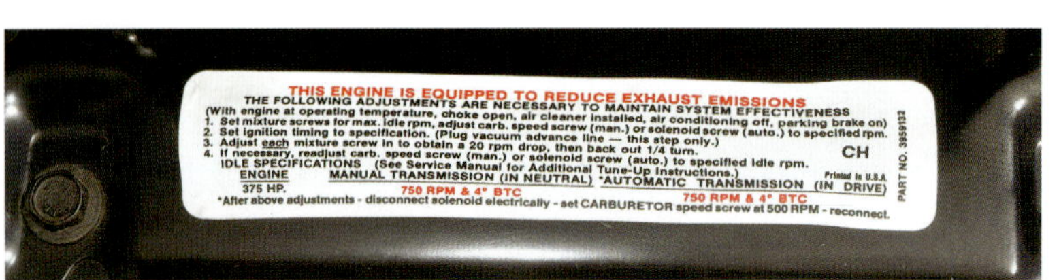

With the extended production of the 1969 model year well into August 1969, over half a million 1969 Chevelles were built. With reported sales of 86,307 SS 396-optioned cars, 1969 saw more SS 396 Chevelles than any year that it was a series or option, having more than 14,000 more in sales than the next-closest year for the series or option. Maybe you, your neighbor, or the counter guy at the hot rod shop had one.

CHEVELLE CLUBS AND SHOWS

Chevrolet's Chevelle is unquestionably one of the most popular (if not *the* most popular) midsize car produced in the mid-1960s and early 1970s. There are probably Chevelle clubs in every state, and some states have multiple clubs. Many of these Chevelle clubs host at least one Chevelle show a year and will have between 100 and 200 Chevelles of the classic era (1964–1972) in attendance. While most attendees are the ever-popular sport coupe and convertible bodystyles, sedans, sedan pickups, and station wagons are welcomed and often present as well. Entrants range from original survivor Chevelles to restored-back-to-original, *Day 2* modified Chevelles and highly modified Chevelles. There are typically classes for each variant at these shows.

DAY 2 CHEVELLES

Typical modifications to modern Day 2 Chevelles include modern or classic custom wheels (often with reproductions of original-style tires), additional gauges (such as tachometer and oil pressure/

The 1969 model year is growing in popularity and typically coming very close to the number of 1970 attendees. The Northern Ohio Chevelle Club show honored the 1969 Chevelle for its 50th anniversary with 100 1969 Chevelles in attendance.

volt/water temperature gauges), maybe a splash of extra chrome accessories under the hood, modern air-conditioning, and personal touches.

Back in the day, many of these Chevelles were the main transportation for their owners and saw a lot of miles being accumulated in simple commuting duties. On many occasions, the owners would test their mettle on local drag strips. Consequently, a lot of original parts were replaced over time due to wearing out or racing breakage. Today, there are enough replacement pieces in the aftermarket world that a Chevelle can be dragged from an old barn and rebuilt into a reliable driver or show car. Original cars with correct, date-coded pieces and known history are highly sought out.

THE 1970s SLUMP

With the fuel crunch and industry downplaying the horsepower wars in 1973, many of the high-horsepower Chevelles were bought for a song. Insurance companies were beginning to charge pre-mium rates for performance cars around the same time. Weather conditions from Mother Nature had a hand in the demise of quality cars, causing rust issues.

Those that did survive the day-to-day driving duties and harsh weather began to come back into vogue in the early 1980s and began to hit the streets and local car shows again. Previous Chevelle owners who gave up their cars due to military service, starting a family, etc. began seeking out their old Chevelles —or something as close to it as they could find. Owners began stripping Day 2 cars of their owner-added adornments either at home as a project or having a quality restorer do much of the work, and they began seeking original, proper date-coded parts to return them back to factory-delivered condition.

CHRIS TOTH: SS 396

By Chris Toth

I bought my 1969 Chevelle from a friend who had purchased the car in 2002. He hadn't done anything with it, and

Chris's relatively rare Burnished Brown SS 396 is outfitted with a Parchment vinyl top and matching Parchment interior. The car is optioned with some relatively rare items, such as the Traction Compound and Dispenser (278 units sold) and the Lamp Monitoring system (2,041 units sold). (Photo Courtesy Chris Toth)

1969 Chevrolet Chevelle SS 396
In Detail No. 12

when I visited him on several occasions, I couldn't see the diamond in the rough until I bought another 1969. I started noticing how much better the panel fitment and gaps were on my friend's Chevelle than mine. I noticed the options that it had and emailed Dale to ask him what the canisters were in the trunk and the lamps on the front fenders. Dale told me the canisters were a rare option: RPO V75 Traction Compound and Dispenser. The lamps on the fenders were the RPO U46 Lamp Monitoring System.

After looking at all the options and panel gaps on my friend's car, I realized that I had to sell my Chevelle and buy this solid car, and that is what I did in 2015. The next three to four years were used to restore the car back to its original Burnished Brown and Parchment vinyl top and interior.

My friend had traded the bench seat for bucket seats, but I found the gentleman who had the original bench seat and gave him a call. Eight years after the initial trade, I traded the bucket seats back for the bench seat.

A few things still need to be done to bring my car back to its original condition. First and foremost on the list is to restore the air-conditioning back to its working state.

SAM GRIFFITH: L78 SS 396

By Sam Griffith

I first saw my SS at the Pavillions car show near Scottsdale, Arizona, in 2003. I recently moved to Arizona, and a new friend pointed it out to me in a sea of wonderful cars. What stood out for me in his description was "L78, 4-speed, original black paint and red interior, 30,000 miles, and original cancelled check from the 1969 purchase."

I had to check this out for myself, and that evening I met the then owner, Stan Harvell. It didn't take long for me to realize that this Chevelle was destined to be part of my future. Fast-forward to January 2006, and I completed the deal with Stan and happily drove the car home to my shop.

Besides the obvious attributes of this solid-lifter Chevelle, I believe what has truly made ownership of this car special was getting to know the original owner, Wayne Tuck, who still resides in the same town where he bought it at age 20 in June 1969. He has filled in all of the gaps of this Chevelle's storied past, whether

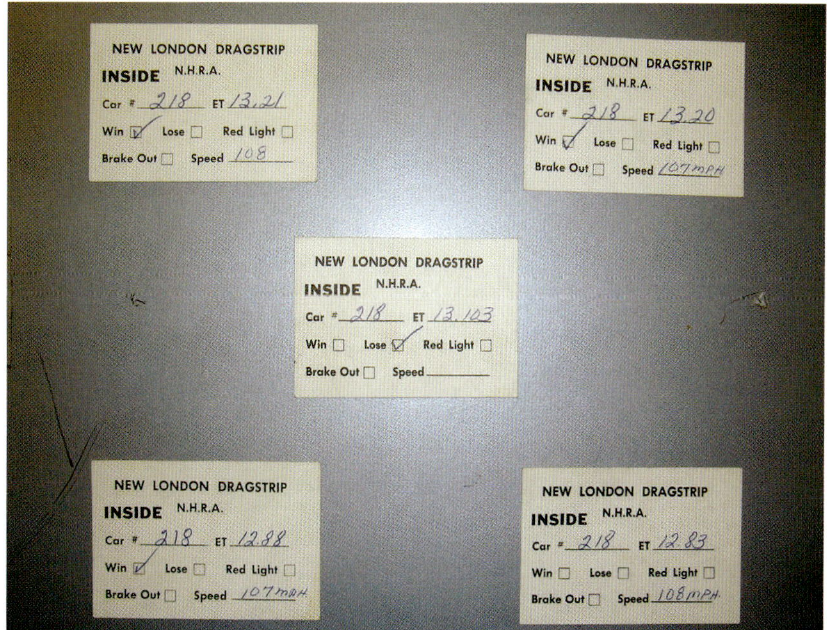

Sam Griffith displays vintage drag racing time slips for his car from New London Dragstrip. His L78 Chevelle ran in the low 13s to high 12s at 107 to 108 mph back in the day. Trap speeds and elapsed times were typical of the day for Sam's Chevelle. (Photo Courtesy Sam Griffith)

The combination of period-correct Mickey Thompson finned-aluminum rocker-arm covers, Mr. Gasket wing nuts, a Lynx Ram-Flo air-filter assembly, and a Mallory ignition and coil was a hot setup. Note the absence of heater hoses from the engine to the heater box. Who needed a heater when you're racing? (Photo Courtesy Sam Griffith)

Gracing Sam's interior is an aftermarket Hurst Competition Plus 4-speed shifter (with the obligatory Hurst T-Handle and super boot) and period-correct Stewart Warner amp, water temperature, and oil pressure gauges. (Photo Courtesy Sam Griffith)

it is street racing or winning trophies at southern Virginia drag strips. He loves to recount his many exploits with his faithful mount. He took such good care of it that it still has most of its original paint, and the factory drivetrain remains in place.

Documented? Yeah, Wayne kept almost every original document, including 1969 VA license plates, the dealership plate frame, keys, dealership order form, title, first insurance policy, car invoice, Protect-O-Plate, warranty paperwork, drag strip time slips, racing trophies, lots of late 1960s/early 1970s photographs, and more. The stories that Wayne recalled were so colorful to me that I submitted an article to *Hemmings Muscle Machines*, and Wayne's Chevelle graced the July 2008 cover as the feature article.

Within the last year, I have returned my Chevelle to its original Day 2, as-raced

configuration based on conversations with Wayne and the many photos that he saved. This included original Mickey Thompson Super Scavenger headers, Stewart Warner gauges, Hurst shifter, Lakewood lower control arms, Gabriel Hi-Jacker shocks, Mallory ignition, and Cragar SS skinnies up front with M&H cheater slicks out back.

I have had quite a few muscle cars over the years, but this has always been my favorite in large part due to its remarkable history. It really draws attention at gas stations and local car shows. Driving it is a real pleasure, particularly rowing the gears and sitting in the original cockpit. The smells, the sounds, the sensations—it's not just a muscle machine, it is a time machine!

RICK NELSON: 427 YENKO

By Rick Nelson

Our 1 of 7 Garnet Red 1969 Yenko Chevelle was located in the original owner's garage where it sat for 47 years after a questionable front accident sidelined the car. It was almost completely disassembled with parts strewn throughout the garage.

In late 2017, we were contacted by the owners' estate with regards to performing a full restoration for them or finding a buyer for the car. I told them that I needed several photos and an asking price for the car. I honestly did not give it much thought.

While eating dinner with my girlfriend, Annie Hartweg, (who herself has owned many high-dollar Chevrolets), we found out that one of our many restoration cus-

tomers might be interested in the car for which we would get the restoration. She proceeded to throw her fork at me and told me to get off my (rear) and go get the damn car. Not having the immediate funds to do so, she stated that she would buy the car, and I would do the restoration. That started the wheel rolling and almost two years of no time off or sleep.

In November 2017 (only days later), we purchased the car and brought it home, where we proceeded to start a full restoration of every component, nut, and bolt using only the best parts and NOS or original pieces that were on the car.

In June 2019, we completed the restoration in our shop with the bodywork and paint going to Super Car Restoration in Clymer, Pennsylvania. No expense was spared, and a total of 2,200 hours of labor was spent on the car during the 19-month period of working on it in the evening hours and on weekends due to a resto-

Annie and Rick's Yenko has the 9737LD Sports Car Conversion that included the 15-inch rally wheels and G70-15 Goodyear Wide Tread GT tires along with the Yenko-unique hood stripes and side stripes. (Photo Courtesy Rick Nelson)

ration business we were running.

We restore cars for a living, and while Annie has owned her share of very rare Chevrolets, I have kept my money in the business. In all my years, I never dreamed that we would own a Yenko Chevelle, but on that day, all the stars seemed to align. Now that we do, it's time to enjoy it for years to come.

ROGER DAY (ORIGINAL OWNER): 427 COPO/ DICK HARRELL CHEVELLE

By Roger Day

It was August 19, 1969. I was on my way to work just before 8 a.m. when I spotted a bright orange Chevelle with black hood stripes on Bill Allen Chevrolet's lot. As I pulled up, Allen's salesman, Charlie Fieden, didn't waste any time. He hit the key points about performance mods at Dick Harrell's shop. A couple of hours later, I drove that brand-new 1969 COPO 427-ci/ Dick Harrell 450-hp Chevelle on to work a few blocks down the street at Whitaker Cable!

I never took the Chevelle to a dragstrip. However, street racing? Absolutely. My first race with classmate John Carter was in early December 1969 on Highway 33 near Plattsburg, Missouri. John had a hot 396 Chevy Nova SS with a few key mods. John smoked his tires off the line, while I screamed to the turnaround. It was a hollow victory—my motor scuffed a cylinder wall and was replaced under GM warranty at Bill Allen's shop a few days later. Just over a year later, the CE warranty replacement engine starved for oil (the oil pickup tube fell off the oil pump into the pan). GM offered a warranty repair but would not replace the failed engine. I traded it while in the shop for a new 1970 Camaro RS, but the Chevelle never left my mind over the years.

My wife and I often talked about the summer of 1970 when we met and about the Monaco Orange '69 Chevelle that was so much a part of that summer. We were having one of those conversations in October 2008 about times past. I decided to do my best to either find the car or chase it to ground.

Success! In August 2009, I tracked it down, and a few days later it was back home and a major restoration effort began.

In June 2011, it looked just as it had on that August 1969 day that I bought it new. During my search and afterward, I

Roger Day is the original owner if this Monaco Orange non-SS 396 Chevelle sports a Parchment interior, 3-speed Turbo Hydra-matic transmission and a Dick Harrell Performance Center-built 427-ci 450-hp engine. Hood stripes and hood key lock pins complete the look. (Photo Courtesy Roger Day)

managed to track down all six subsequent registered owners and the two owners who didn't register it. The orange Chevelle "was really fast," according to those six registered owners. So, I'm not the only one to have street raced this car.

ROBERT KILLINGSWORTH: L78 SS 396

By Robert Killingsworth

My SS 396 Chevelle was discovered and purchased after I spotted it setting in front of a house back in 1985. After some research, I contacted the previous owners and learned of the car's history. It was a true L78 4-speed SS with 4.10:1 gears, and it had been raced on local drag strips in the 1970s. However, it had been neglected and needed some TLC.

A frame-off restoration brought it to its current condition, and it has earned many awards over the past 30-plus years. Now, when the engine roars to life and

the clutch engages, each shift reminds me of a time when these cars roamed the streets and competed on the strip. My current plans are to maintain and enjoy this car for a long time.

DONNIE EDMOND: *BIG BERTHA*

By Donnie Edmond

I found the car for sale on the internet. I was very interested in it, but by the

Robert has owned his L78-optioned Garnet Red SS 396 for more than 30 years and attends many Chevelle car shows in the Midwest regularly. His car is seen here shod with Day 2 Cragar S/S wheels and modern Firestone Wide Oval tires.

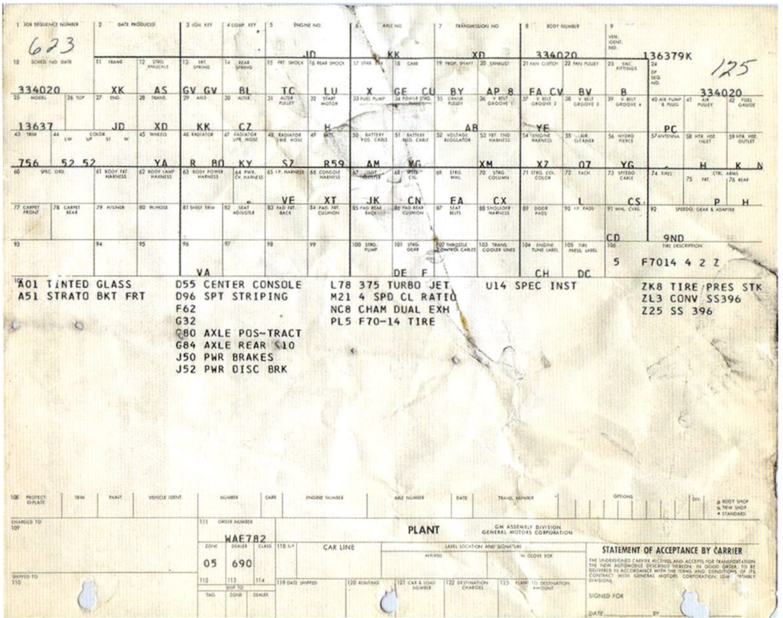

Robert's build sheet shows desirable options beyond the L78 engine: bucket seats, an M21 Muncie close-ratio 4-speed transmission, a 4.10:1 rear gear ratio, special instrumentation, and chambered dual exhaust. (Photo Courtesy Robert Killingsworth)

time I contacted the guy who had it, he told me that he already traded the car away. Lo and behold, a short period of

Donnie Edmonds's all-steel, 565-ci *Big Bertha* 1969 Chevelle easily pulls the front wheels off the drag strip on its way to another sub 10-second run. The 500-plus-ci big-block makes this an easy task. (Photo Courtesy Donnie Edmonds)

time later, the car was back on the net, and I contacted the guy who had it and made plans to look at the car. I called the guy to let him know that I was planning to go to Chicago that weekend to look at the car, when he told me that he traded it.

I had started looking at other cars, and I was ready to make a trip down South to buy another 1969 Chevelle, when I was looking through racing junk, and there it was for sale again. I called the guy and told him that I wanted the car and that I was heading to Crystal Lake, Illinois, that weekend to pick it up. During that phone call, I was told that the drivetrain and interior had been removed and all that was for sale was a gutted body: no engine, transmission, or interior. The wiring was a mess, but the car was very solid and retained all of its original sheet metal except for the hood.

Since I wanted to build a car and not just buy someone else's build, my wife and I drove up, looked the car over, and made the deal. My plan at the time was to have a 9-second all-steel OEM-appearing car. I started collecting parts for the car: a 555-ci big-block, a TH400 transmission, new electronics, and more. One friend had a set of Chevelle bucket seat frames, and another had a rear seat.

Long story short, over the winter of

2013–2014, I was able to get the car back together, and by June 2014, the car made its first 9-second pass with a 9.97 at 132 mph. Since that time, many changes have been made: 6 different engines, 11 transmissions, and a new suspension and anti-roll bar.

Last October, I had Straub Technologies and Foxwell Motorsports plan and build a 565-ci big-block to make my final assault on the 9.00 barrier.

In September 2009, I decided to go for my goal. The car weighed in at 3,700 pounds with driver. It still had all-steel construction (except for the hood), a full factory interior, a 100-percent uncut and unmodified body with nothing more than bolt-on parts, and 10.5-inch tires. At 3,000 feet density altitude, 100 ppm water grains, and 87°F, the car went its quickest and fastest (9.161 at 146.77 mph) at the National Muscle Car Association (NMCA) race in Indy. I am more than confident the car has an 8.90 in it once I get some good air and track conditions.

BOB TERRY: 496-CI BIG-BLOCK

Bob Terry's 1969 Chevelle features a 496-ci big-block, a TH-400 transmission, and a Ford 9-inch rear end with 4.11:1 gears. Bob's car weighs 4,035 pounds with a full interior, spare tire, and driver.

DUSTIN HERBISON: OSHAWA SS 396

By Dustin Herbison

My uncle purchased the car used from Dueck Chevrolet in Vancouver, British Columbia, in 1970. At the time, it had 5,000 miles on the odometer. My father, Dwight, purchased the car in 1973 from his brother. Dwight enjoyed the car through his last year of high school in Kamloops, British Columbia, but soon after, he found himself working in a mining camp in the Northwest Territories. During this time, the car sat at his parents' house, occasionally being driven by his mother.

By 1983, Dwight brought the car up to the Northwest Territories, where he met his wife and started a family. He spent most of his free time in the 1980s flying his airplane. The car was barely driven and sat mainly idle for three years in his airplane hangar.

By 1987, Dwight's family had moved to the small town of Cawston, British Columbia, and the Chevelle came along, finding a resting place in the garage. The rumor mill brought forth a few potential buyers in the 1990s, but Dwight wasn't willing to part with the car. It was parked in the garage in daily-driver condition until 2002. At that time, it was restored by Dwight and me to its current condition.

Bob Terry's gold 1969 Chevelle squares off at an NMCA event with another 1969 Chevelle. Bob is a regular competitor at NMCA events and has been known to yank the front wheels a time or two. Bob's Chevelle has run a best of 11.26 seconds at 117 mph to date. (Photo Courtesy Cliff Copeland)

Early Oshawa-built SS 396 Chevelles began their VIN sequencing with 100001 and still had *M A L I B U* script on the rear quarter panels. Oshawa-built SS 396 Chevelles did not begin using the US sequencing of 300001 until January 1969, and the script was removed at that time as well. (Photo Courtesy Dustin Herbison)

In 2013, Dwight was contacted by fellow Chevelle enthusiast Gary Templeman, who had seen a picture of the car on a website forum. Gary had a 1969 Chevelle SS 396 hardtop. After comparing notes, it was discovered that both cars had a starting sequence number beginning with 100001 and were built on the same day in September 1968, only a few cars apart on the Oshawa assembly line. Both cars had the quarter panel Malibu script, a detail that often led to speculation by others that Dwight's car was simply a Malibu that was fitted with SS 396 badging.

Today, the car is collector-plated and lovingly enjoyed by Dwight and his family.

LOOKING TO THE FUTURE

Men and women today have settled families, the kids are grown and gone, and they are still looking for their first Chevelle or at least one to replace their car from 50 years ago. This desire has fueled the aftermarket for everything from body panels to interior trim, badging, engine accessories, wheels, tires, etc. to recreate the Chevelle of their dreams. A number of outlets are available for Chevelle parts and accessories today to help make those dreams come true.

Factory Appearing Stock Tire (FAST) is one of several racing events for muscle cars of the 1960s and 1970s (primarily stock cars of the era). NMCA drag racing events are pretty much open to *run what ya brung.*

PAINT CHARTS, OPTIONS, VIN AND TRIM TAG DECODER, AND PRODUCTION NUMBERS

PRODUCTION NUMBERS BY SERIES/BODYSTYLE

The production numbers shown here are from GM production reports. These are the five possible series/bodystyles that could have ordered the RPO Z25 SS 396 Equipment option.

Series, Bodystyle	Fisher Bodystyle Number	Quantity Sold
300 Deluxe two-door coupe	13427	5,620
300 Deluxe two-door sport coupe	13437	7,181
Malibu sport coupe	13637	286,162
Malibu convertible	13667	8,443
Malibu two-door sedan pickup	13680	39,000
Total possible production of SS 396		346,406

PRODUCTION NUMBERS BY PLANT

Although there are production numbers for each plant as reported by General Motors, there are no numbers for specific series or bodystyles. Some plants can be eliminated for bodystyles, such as the sedan pickup, which was only built at the Baltimore, Fremont, and Kansas City final assembly plants. Neither Atlanta or Framingham built convertibles or station wagons.

Month	Atlanta-A	Baltimore-B	Framingham-G
September	300001-302597	300001-308846	300001-304912
October	302598-306613	308847-318059	304913-311621
November	306614-310620	318060-326003	311622-317607
December	310621-313846	326004-333025	317608-322570
January	313847-322002	333026-344660	322571-329012
February	322003-329430	344661-355330	329013-333080
March	329431-337539	355331-367113	333081-338712
April	337540-344438	367114-378593	338713-348045
May	no production reported	348594-381442	348046-352264
June	no production reported	381443-396474	352265-360909
July	344439-346616	396475-413729	360910-367942
August	346617-356386	413730-414385	no production reported
Total by plant	56,386	114,385	67,942
Percentage	10.79%	21.88%	13.00%

Month	Fremont-Z	Kansas City-K	Oshawa-1
September	300001-304595	300001-316556	no production reported
October	304596-311759	316557-339096	no production reported
November	311760-319029	339097-358979	no production reported
December	319030-323994	358980-374064	no production reported
January	323995-330138	374065-393881	300001-305317
February	330139-335464	393882-409027	305318-310442
March	335465-341235	409028-425254	310443-315261
April	341236-347446	425255-439077	315262-320566
May	347447-353627	439078-442908	320567-327938
June	353628-360184	442909-461711	327939-334650
July	360185-368119	461712-480619	334651-334765
August	no production reported	480620-481164	no production reported
Total by plant	68,119	181,164	34,765
Percentage	13.03%	34.66%	6.65%

A couple of things should be noted. The Oshawa, Ontario, final assembly plant built 1969 model year Chevelles from September 1968 through December 1968. At least 817 1969 Chevelles have been documented being built at the Oshawa, Ontario, final assembly plant through December 1968. All of these early Oshawa Chevelles have VIN sequence numbers starting with 1xxxxx; the 3xxxxx sequencing did not begin until January 1, 1969.

DECODE YOUR VIN

Unlike previous years, the VIN will provide no indication of the SS 396 Equipment option on a 1969 Chevelle because the SS 396 Equipment was just that, an option. The only data that *could* be an SS 396 Equipment–optioned Chevelle is shown here.

First Character: Division of General Motors
1: Chevrolet division

Second and Third Characters: Series Designation
34: 300 Deluxe, V-8
36: Malibu, V-8

Fourth and Fifth Characters: Bodystyle/Model
27: Two-door coupe (300 Deluxe series only)
37: Two-door sport coupe
67: Two-door convertible
80: Two-door sedan pickup

Sixth Character: Model Year of Production
9: 1969

Seventh Character: Final Assembly Plant Designation
A: Atlanta, Georgia
B: Baltimore, Maryland
G: Framingham, Massachusetts
Z: Fremont, California
K: Kansas City, Missouri
1: Oshawa, Ontario, Canada

Eighth through 13th Characters: Sequential Production Number
The sequential starting number for the 1969 Chevelle was 300001 at all Chevelle assembly plants except as noted above for the Oshawa, Ontario, final assembly plant. Each assembly plant sequenced Chevelles of all series/models without regard to specific series/models. For example, if a series 13435 station wagon followed a 13667 Malibu convertible, the sequence number was one unit higher for the wagon. It's also entirely possible to have the same sequence number from all five 1969 US assembly plants (six if you include Oshawa, Ontario) with the only difference between the VINs being the plant code.

1969 Chevrolet Chevelle SS 396

In Detail No. 12

ENGINE SUFFIX CODES

The engine's two- or three-letter suffix code is used to specify the horsepower rating and transmission type to be used.

Code	HP-RPO	Transmission	Notes
JA	325-L35	Manual	A.I.R.
JC	350-L34	Manual	A.I.R.
JD	375-L78	Manual	A.I.R.
JE	350-L34	TH400	A.I.R.
JK	325-L35	TH400	C.C.S.
JV	325-L35	Manual	A.I.R./H.D. clutch
KB	350-L34	Manual	A.I.R./H.D. clutch
KD	375-L78	Manual	A.I.R./H.D. clutch
KF	375-L78	TH400	A.I.R.
KG	375-L78/L89	Manual	A.I.R./L89 aluminum head
KH	375-L78/L89	TH400	A.I.R./L89 aluminum head
KI	375-L78/L89	Manual	A.I.R./H.D. clutch/L89 aluminum head

In late 1969, all 396-ci engines were being bored to 402-ci in anticipation of the 1970 model year. The 1969 versions of these engines used the same suffix codes with the letter *C* preceding the code, such as *CJA, CJC, CJD*, etc.

SPECIAL PAINT (RPO ZP3)

DuPont Mixing Formula	Color
926-93253	Orange
926-97249	Red
926-96371	Light Blue (often called Carolina Blue)
926-99568	Yellow (Daytona Yellow)
926-99616	Orange (Hugger/Monaco Orange often referred to as "Road Commission Orange")

PAINT CODES AND SALES NAMES

Paint codes for 1969 changed from a letter to a 2-digit number when displayed on the Fisher Body Number Plate (a.k.a. trim tag). Internal RPO paint codes differed from those depicted on the trim tag and were a 3-digit number and a 2-letter code.

Paint Code	Sales Name	RPO Paint Name (Code)
10	Tuxedo Black	black (910AA)
40	Butternut Yellow	yellow (916YY)
50	Dover White	white (911CC)
51	Dusk Blue	dark blue (923EE)
52	Garnet Red	red (913RR)
53	Glacier Blue	blue (922DD)
55	Azure Turquoise	turquoise (921KK)
57	Fathom Green	dark green (920VV)
59	Frost Green	lime (919WW)
61	Burnished Brown	dark brown (918SS)
63	Champagne	champagne (917MM)
65	Olympic Gold	gold (915GG)
67	Burgundy	maroon (914NN)
69	Cortez Silver	silver (912BB)
71	LeMans Blue	bright blue (924FF)
72	Monaco/Hugger Orange	orange (927QQ)
76	Daytona Yellow	bright yellow (926PP)
53/50	Glacier Blue/Dover White	blue/white (954DC)
53/51	Glacier Blue/Dusk Blue	blue/dark blue (955DE)
51/53	Dusk Blue/Glacier Blue	dark blue/blue (956ED)
65/50	Olympic Gold/Dover White	gold/white (957GC)
55/50	Azure Turquoise/Dover White	turquoise/white (958KC)
61/63	Burnished Brown/Champagne	dark brown/champagne (959SM)

Any SS 396 Equipment–optioned Chevelle could be ordered in any of the colors above, including two-tone combinations on coupes and sport coupes only.

Although not broken down by specific series or model identification, the popularity of the various colors offered may come as a surprise to some. To date, there is no known breakdown of a color and series or body-styles, nor was how many of any color ordered on a convertible or in combination with a vinyl top.

Popularity Number	Total Reported Sales	Color (Sales Name)
1	81,883	Frost Green*
2	51,060	LeMans Blue
3	44,118	Olympic Gold
4	41,226	Fathom Green
5	36,377	Glacier Blue
6	33,152	Dover White
7	29,449	Garnet Red
8	27,028	Butternut Yellow
9	23,610	Champagne
10	22,980	Azure Turquoise
11	20,419	Cortez Silver
12	19,230	Dusk Blue
13	17,724	Burnished Brown
14	14,415	Burgundy
15	7,441	Tuxedo Black
16	5,194	Hugger/Monaco Orange**
17	3,465	Special & Prime
18	2,841	Daytona Yellow**

*Also called Frost Lime in some Chevelle documentation.

**Only available with RPO Z25 SS 396 Equipment option. These two colors could be ordered on any 1969 Chevelle but were reflected in the "Special & Prime" category.

Popularity Number	Two-Tone	Colors (Lower/Upper)
1	5,658	Burnished Brown/Champagne
2	5,057	Olympic Gold/Dover White
3	4,754	Azure Turquoise/Dover White
4	4,590	Glacier Blue/Dover White
5	883	Dusk Blue/Glacier Blue
6	798	Glacier Blue / Dusk Blue

CONVERTIBLE/VINYL TOP COLORS

Convertible top colors were limited to white (RPO C05AA) or black (RPO C05BB), and either color could be ordered with any of the 17 body colors. A white convertible top was standard, and black was a no-cost choice. A vinyl top was optional and available in five different colors: Black, Parchment, Dark Blue, Dark Brown, and Midnight Green. The suggested vinyl top colors with specific lower body colors are shown in these tables:

Vinyl Top Color	Suggested Lower Body Colors
Black (C08BB)	Any body color
Parchment (C08EE)	Any body color
Dark Blue (C08CC)	Dover White, Cortez Silver, Glacier Blue, and Dusk Blue
Dark Brown (C08FF)	Olympic Gold, Butternut Yellow, Champagne, and Burnished Brown
Midnight Green (C08GG*)	Tuxedo Black, Dover White, Frost Green, and Fathom Green

*Midnight Green has been found with letter code "G" and "S" on a trim tag.

A vinyl top was optional on any Chevelle coupe, sport coupe, sedan, sport sedan, or sedan pickup and was not limited to an SS 396 Equipment–optioned Chevelle.

Any deviation from the suggested combinations would require a F&SO change.

OPTIONS

Aside from various RPO items that were part of the SS 396 Equipment–option package, there are very few options that an SS 396 Equipment–optioned Chevelle could opt for that could not be ordered as an individual option by any other Chevelle. Aside from some obvious options (such as the Powerglide automatic transmission, hubcaps or wheel covers, and station wagon–specific items, including the roof luggage carrier, electric tailgate window, etc.) RPO F41 Special Performance Front and Rear Suspension was only available as an option on SS 396 Equipment–optioned 300 Deluxe coupes and sport coupes as well as Malibu sport coupes and convertibles. This was still an option in 1969 and did not become standard equipment on an SS-optioned Chevelle until the 1970 model year, and only 772 RPO F41 options were sold in 1969. The sedan pickup was not a candidate for RPO F41 due to the sedan pickup having standard rear air shocks. RPO D96 Accent Stripe was available with any 300 Deluxe coupe or sport coupe and Malibu-series sport coupe, convertible, or sedan pickup ordered with the SS 396 Equipment option. RPO U14 special instrumentation was available with any V-8 300 Deluxe coupe or sport coupe and Malibu-series sport coupe, convertible, or sedan pickup. Some standard SS 396 Equipment–option items, such as JL2/J50 power disc brakes, could be ordered on any Chevelle, and dual exhaust was an option on both the L65 and L48 engines

A number of items in the SS 396 Equipment–option package were unique to the SS 396 Equipment option and not available as options on any non-SS 396 Equipment optioned Chevelle:
- RPO D96 Accent Stripe
- RPO F41 Special Performance Front and Rear (not available on the sedan pickup)
- RPO 927QQ Hugger/Monaco Orange and RPO 926PP Daytona Yellow paint

The SS 396 Equipment option included appropriate SS 396 badging on the front fenders, the rear tail panel, door panels, and dash trim. Some items were removed from the non-SS optioned Malibu sport coupe/convertible/sedan pickup when the SS 396 Equipment option was ordered, such as the bright side molding with Argent Silver paint below the molding and front side marker lamps with the V-8 engine size designation. The molding was replaced with a shorter, 300 Deluxe–series side grille molding (even on the Malibu series) and front side marker lamps with no engine size designation. There were subtle changes, such as the parking lamp lens getting a bright outside trim ring. On SS 396 Equipment–optioned sedan pickups, the panel between the bright trim was blacked out on the tailgate. When a 300 Deluxe was ordered with the SS 396 Equipment option, it received the Malibu taillamp assembly, the bright trim, and a blacked-out rear panel and SS 396 badging.

Also included with RPO Z25 was the 325-hp 396-ci engine with bright accents (rocker-arm covers, oil filler cap, and air-cleaner housing lid), a heavy-duty man-ual 3-speed floor-shifted transmission, dual exhausts, a black-painted grille and rear panel, wheel-opening moldings, special hood, 14x7 sport wheels with F70-14 white-lettered blackwall tires, and power front disc brakes. GM's documentation indicates the sedan pickup with the SS 396 Equipment option was to get G70-14 tires, and several Fremont build sheets and shipping documents show just that. Other GM documentation indicates the SS Equipment–optioned sedan pickup was to receive F70-14 tires. Both white-stripe and red-stripe tires were available as options in both F70-14 and G70-14 sizes: F70-14 white stripe (RPO PW7) and red stripe (RPO PW8), and G70-14 white stripe (RPO PX8) and red stripe (RPO PY7).

SS EMBLEMS

An SS emblem was substituted on the standard SS 396 Equipment–optioned steering wheel in lieu of the blue bowtie or Malibu script. All standard SS 396 Equip-ment–optioned steering wheels were black regardless of interior trim color. The grille of both SS 396 Equip-ment options included a single SS emblem with no engine size noted. The front fenders removed the side marker and engine size designation and replaced it with a simple side marker. SS 396 emblems were also used to replace the Malibu emblem on the front door panels of the Malibu sport coupe and convertible on SS 396-optioned Chevelles. The SS 396 emblems were never used in the sedan pickup door panels (due to the vent wing regulator handle) or on the 300 Deluxe door panels.

SS 396 EQUIPMENT–OPTION TIRES

The SS 396 Equipment–optioned 300 Deluxe coupe and sport coupe, as well as the Malibu sport coupe and convertible, have F70-14 raised white-letter tires as stan-dard equipment, while the SS 396 Equipment–optioned sedan pickup received slightly larger G70-14 tires early on at some plants. Both white-stripe and red-stripe tires were available as options in both F70-14 and G70-14 sizes: F70-14 white stripe (RPO PW7) and red stripe (RPO PW8), and G70-14 white stripe (RPO PX8) and red stripe (RPO PY7).

INTERIOR

Non-cloth seats in 1969 are described as *coated fabric* instead of the previous years' description of *imitation leather* or *vinyl*. For the sake of continuity and to quell confusion, the term *vinyl* is used here as well. Cloth/vinyl bench seats were standard for all Malibu sport coupes (for most colors), while vinyl-only bench seats were standard for all Malibu convertibles and sedan pickups. The SS 396 Equipment option had no bearing on the base seat material. The 300 Deluxe seats were only available in black, blue, and green. Bucket seats were not an option in the 300 Deluxe, even when the SS 396 Equipment option was ordered. The all-vinyl bench seats were a $12.65 option in Malibu sport coupes but standard in convertibles and sedan pickups. All seven bucket seat colors were all vinyl, and all bucket seats were a $121.15 option. Several bucket seat colors were only available with specific Malibu-series bodystyles.

Bucket Seats			
Trim Code	Seat Color	Series/Bodystyle	Quantity
756	Black	13637, 13667, 13680	44,252
765	Metallic Dark Blue	13637, 13667, 13680	7,502
771	Antique Medium Saddle	13680	707
785	Metallic Medium Green	13637	3,516
788	Medium Red	13637, 13667	2,358
791	Parchment	13637, 13667	13,140
796	Midnight Green	13637	8,383

QUIRKS

General Motors of Canada built Chevelles in 1969 with the exception of the sedan pickup bodystyle. The SS 396 Equipment option was certainly available, but

General Motors of Canada's early SS Equipment-optioned Malibus retained the *M A L I B U* script on the quarter panels. It is not known just when this practice ended at the Oshawa plant, but it was at least through VIN 111,323 with a delivery date of December 28, 1968. (Photo Courtesy Dustin Herbison)

only the base L35 325-hp and optional L34 350-hp engines were available. If a buyer wanted the 375-hp L78 engine, the car was built in the US and shipped to a Canadian dealer. Early Malibu-series SS 396 Equipment–optioned Chevelles built in Canada retained the *M A L I B U* script on the rear quarter panels as well. It isn't known just when this practice ended, but research has turned up four to date. Also, early Canadian-built Chevelles have sequence numbers starting with 100,001 instead of the more-common 300,001. Again, it is not known just how many early 1969 Canadian-built Chevelles have a sequence number in the 1xx,xxx range, but research has turned up 111,323 as the highest found to date.

Partial VIN Stamp

Along with the engine block (and often the frame), the firewall often contained what is commonly called a partial VIN, CONVIN (or concealed VIN), or VIN derivative. This example is for Atlanta. No partial VINs include the series or bodystyle. They only include the General Motors division identifier (1), model year (9), assembly plant designation letter (A in this instance), and the 6-digit sequence number. This partial VIN stamp will match the one on the frame and the firewall behind the heater box to insure that the car has not been rebodied.

1969 Chevrolet Chevelle SS 396
In Detail No. 12

Typically, the partial VIN (or VIN derivative) was stamped on the engine pad in front of the passenger-side cylinder head with the Tonawanda engine plant date and engine identification. Both the Atlanta, Georgia, and Kansas City, Missouri, assembly plants stamped the partial VIN on the rough cast area by the oil filter. (Photo Courtesy SS 396 Registry)

Both the Atlanta and Kansas City final assembly plants stamped the partial VIN on the rough cast area by the oil filter, while Baltimore, Framingham, and Fremont stamped the partial VIN on the engine pad next to the engine date/suffix code stamp from the Tonawanda engine plant.

SS 396 Body Modifications

Internally, the SS 396 Equipment option was RPO ZL3 SS 396 Conversion, although the verbiage may differ among the assembly plants. Several body modifications were made to both the 300 Deluxe-series and Malibu-series Chevelles. Both series received the normal SS 396 equipment, such as the domed hood, a 396-ci V-8 engine, power front disc brakes, special 3-speed manual floor-shifted transmission, wheel-opening moldings, special suspension (but not the optional F41 suspension package), 14x7 sport wheels, F70-14 white-lettered blackwall tires (or G70-14 white-stripe tires on the El Camino), a blacked out grille/tail panel, and SS 396 badging.

The 300 Deluxe coupe and sport coupe also received the same taillamp assembly and blacked-out tail panel and bright trim as a standard Malibu. Like the Malibu series, the 300 Deluxe coupe and sport coupe also received a black steering wheel with SS emblem and column regardless of interior color. Although the

While Malibu-series Chevelles received an *SS 396* door emblem in lieu of the *Malibu* emblem, neither 300 Deluxe Chevelle received it when optioned with the SS 396 Equipment option.

300 Deluxe series received the *SS 396* nameplate on the instrument panel, it did not get the *SS 396* door emblems. The 300 Deluxe could not be ordered with bucket seats, and the SS 396 Equipment option did nothing to change that, the cloth/vinyl bench seat was the only seating possible with all vinyl being a $12.65 option available in black only. Carpeting was also not an option, and the 300 Deluxe retained the color-coordinated rubberized floor cover.

The Malibu-series sport coupe and convertible changes with the SS 396 Equipment option included the elimination of the extended headlamp eyebrow, associated bright trim on the lower rocker panel, and the Argent Silver paint on the front splash pan and lower rocker area. The front side lamps from the 300 Deluxe series were used, and the V-8 engine size was eliminated.

Chambered Exhaust

Very early 1969 Chevelles with the optional L34 and L78 engines (and those L78 engines with the optional L89 aluminum heads) were equipped with chambered exhaust systems. A Chevrolet Dealer Service Technical Bulletin dated December 23, 1968, notified dealers that the chambered exhaust system would no longer be standard equipment on these engines in Chevelles (and Z28 Camaros) effective on November 25, 1968. This was a result of local and state police issuing warnings and citations to owners for "excessive noise." The chambered exhaust system would remain an option under RPO NC8 for the remainder of the production year.

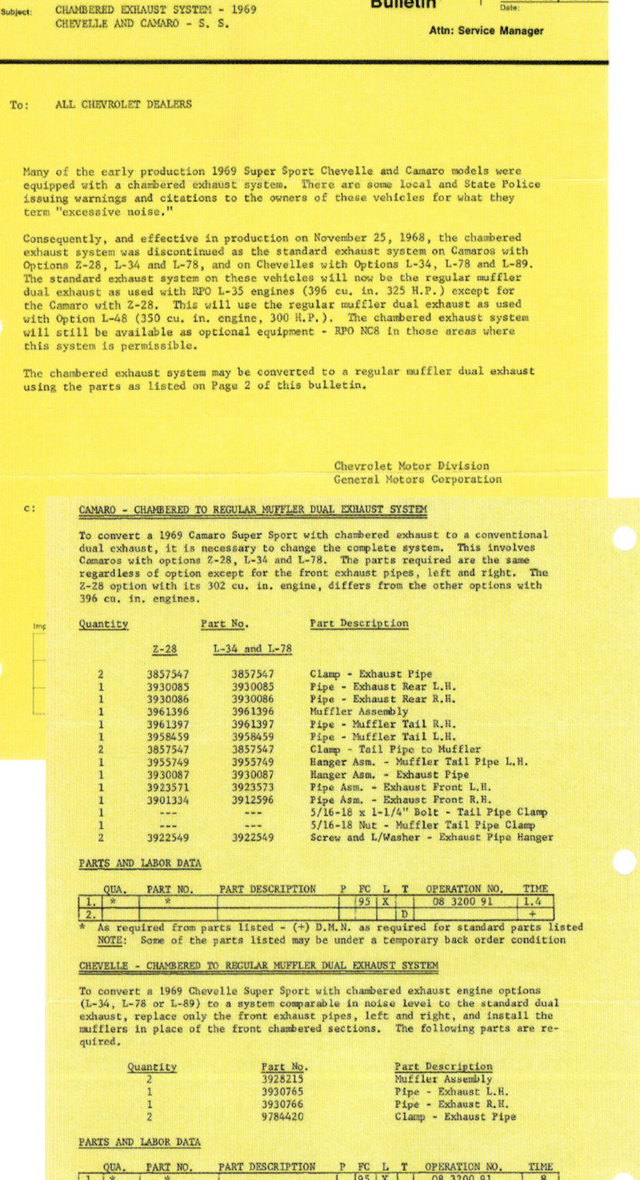

Chevrolet Motor Division
General Motors Corporation
Chevrolet Service Department

Chevrolet Dealer Service Technical Bulletin

Number: 69-T-8
Section: VIII
Date: Dec. 23, 1968

Subject: CHAMBERED EXHAUST SYSTEM - 1969
CHEVELLE AND CAMARO - S. S.

Attn: Service Manager

To: ALL CHEVROLET DEALERS

Many of the early production 1969 Super Sport Chevelle and Camaro models were equipped with a chambered exhaust system. There are some local and State Police issuing warnings and citations to the owners of these vehicles for what they term "excessive noise."

Consequently, and effective in production on November 25, 1968, the chambered exhaust system was discontinued as the standard exhaust system on Camaros with Options Z-28, L-34 and L-78, and on Chevelles with Options L-34, L-78 and L-89. The standard exhaust system on these vehicles will now be the regular muffler dual exhaust as used with RPO L-35 engines (396 cu. in. 325 H.P.) except for the Camaro with Z-28. This will use the regular muffler dual exhaust as used with Option L-48 (350 cu. in. engine, 300 H.P.). The chambered exhaust system will still be available as optional equipment - RPO NC8 in those areas where this system is permissible.

The chambered exhaust system may be converted to a regular muffler dual exhaust using the parts as listed on Page 2 of this bulletin.

Chevrolet Motor Division
General Motors Corporation

CAMARO - CHAMBERED TO REGULAR MUFFLER DUAL EXHAUST SYSTEM

To convert a 1969 Camaro Super Sport with chambered exhaust to a conventional dual exhaust, it is necessary to change the complete system. This involves Camaros with options Z-28, L-34 and L-78. The parts required are the same regardless of option except for the front exhaust pipes, left and right. The Z-28 option with its 302 cu. in. engine, differs from the other options with 396 cu. in. engines.

Quantity	Part No. Z-28	Part No. L-34 and L-78	Part Description
2	3857547	3857547	Clamp - Exhaust Pipe
1	3930085	3930085	Pipe - Exhaust Rear L.H.
1	3930086	3930086	Pipe - Exhaust Rear R.H.
1	3961396	3961396	Muffler Assembly
1	3961397	3961397	Pipe - Muffler Tail R.H.
1	3958459	3958459	Pipe - Muffler Tail L.H.
2	3857547	3857547	Clamp - Tail Pipe to Muffler
1	3955749	3955749	Hanger Asm. - Muffler Tail Pipe L.H.
1	3930087	3930087	Hanger Asm. - Exhaust Pipe
1	3923571	3923573	Pipe Asm. - Exhaust Front L.H.
1	3901334	3912596	Pipe Asm. - Exhaust Front R.H.
1	---	---	5/16-18 x 1-1/4" Bolt - Tail Pipe Clamp
1	---	---	5/16-18 Nut - Muffler Tail Pipe Clamp
2	3922549	3922549	Screw and L/Washer - Exhaust Pipe Hanger

PARTS AND LABOR DATA

	QUA.	PART NO.	PART DESCRIPTION	P	FC	L	T	OPERATION NO.	TIME
1.	*	*			95	X		08 3200 91	1.4
2.							D		+

* As required from parts listed - (+) D.M.N. as required for standard parts listed
NOTE: Some of the parts listed may be under a temporary back order condition

CHEVELLE - CHAMBERED TO REGULAR MUFFLER DUAL EXHAUST SYSTEM

To convert a 1969 Chevelle Super Sport with chambered exhaust engine options (L-34, L-78 or L-89) to a system comparable in noise level to the standard dual exhaust, replace only the front exhaust pipes, left and right, and install the mufflers in place of the front chambered sections. The following parts are required.

Quantity	Part No.	Part Description
2	3928215	Muffler Assembly
1	3930765	Pipe - Exhaust L.H.
1	3930766	Pipe - Exhaust R.H.
2	9784420	Clamp - Exhaust Pipe

PARTS AND LABOR DATA

	QUA.	PART NO.	PART DESCRIPTION	P	FC	L	T	OPERATION NO.	TIME
1.	*	*			95	X		08 3200 91	.8

* As required from parts listed

Option Codes and Units

RPO	Description	Sold	Models
AR1	Less Head Restraint (N/A after 12/31/1968)	774	All
AS1	Shoulder Harness – Standard	45	13667
AS4	Rear Seat Shoulder Harness – Deluxe	91	All except 13680
AS5	Rear Seat Shoulder Harness – Standard	206	All except 13680
A01	Tinted Glass – All	300,035	All
A02	Tinted Glass – Windshield Only	4,470	All
A31	Windows – Electric Control	4,583	13500-800
A39	Custom Deluxe Seat Belts, front & rear	789	13667
A51	Strato-Bucket Seats	79,871	13637-67-80
A85	Deluxe Shoulder Harness	168	13667
A93	Vacuum Operated Door Locks	1,206	All
BX4	Body Side Molding	11,377	All except SS 396
B37	Floor Mats	84,085	All
B90	Door Window Frame Molding	7,633	13427
B93	Door Edge Guards	133,295	All
CE1	Headlamp Washer	562	All
C06	Folding Top Electric Control	6,211	13667
C08	Exterior Soft Trim Roof Cover	201,671	13427-37-13637-80
C24	Hideaway Windshield Wipers*****	706	13427-37
C50	Rear Window Defroster	15,372	13427-37-13637-67
C60	Air Conditioning – Deluxe	168,449	All
D33	Outside Mirror – Remote Control	20,025	All
D34	Vanity Visor Mirror	18,576	All
D55	Front Compartment Console (requires A51)	72,201	All
D96	Wide Paint Stripe – Side (SS only)	37,280	All
F40	Special Front & Rear Suspension	28,748	All
F41	Special Performance Front & Rear Suspension (SS only)	722	13427-37-13637-67
G80	Rear Axle – Positraction	73,397	All
G82	Rear Axle – 4.56:1 Ratio	1	All
G84	Rear Axle – 4.10:1 Ratio	6,250	All
G96	Rear Axle – 3.55:1 Ratio	4,368	All
G97	Rear Axle – 2.73:1 Ratio	1,268	All
H01	Rear Axle – 3.07:1 Ratio	2,369	All
J50	Power Brake Equipment*	86,307*	All
J52	Disc Brakes, Front*	86,307*	All
KD5	Heavy Duty Closed Positive Vent (L35 only)	129	All
K79	42 Amp. Generator – Delcotron (N/A w/L78 or AC)	1,605	All

Chambered exhaust for the Chevelle with either the L34 350-hp 396-ci engine or the L78 375-hp 396-ci engine was discontinued as standard equipment early in the model year. A Chevrolet Dealer Service Technical Bulletin alerted dealers of the change. (Photo Courtesy Robert Killingsworth)

The second page of the Dealer Service Technical Bulletin on the chambered exhaust system shows instructions to dealers on exhaust part numbers to convert the chambered exhaust to standard dual exhaust for the SS 396 Chevelle. (Photo Courtesy Robert Killingsworth)

	Option	Sold	Series/Bodystyle
5	63 Amp. Generator – Delcotron (N/A w/AC)	1,080	All
4	Engine – V-8 – 396-ci High Performance	17,358	All
5	Engine – V-8 – 396-ci (base SS 396)	53,969	All
3	Engine – V-8 – 396-ci Special High Performance	9,468	All
9	Aluminum Cylinder Heads (L78 V-8 only)	400	All
21	Heavy Duty 3-Speed Manual Transmission*	15,728	All
0	4-Speed Transmission (wide ratio)	44,950	All
1	4-Speed Transmission (close ratio)	13,786	All
2	4-Speed Transmission (heavy duty)	1,276	All
0	3-Speed Turbo Hydra-matic Transmission	32,031	All
8	Chambered Exhaust	4,143	All
3	Steering Wheel – Tilt	10,718	All
4	Steering Wheel – Wood-Grain Plastic	7,515	All
0	Power Steering	366,017	All
4	F70-14/B Fiberglass Belt White Letter** ($26.25)	N/A	13427-37-13637-67
7	F70-14/two-ply (four-ply rating) OE White Stripe (n.c.)	19,799	13427-37-13637-67
8	F70-14/two-ply (four-ply rating) OE Red Stripe (n.c.)	6,243	13427-37-13637-67
3	G70-14/B Fiberglass Belt White Stripe** ($25.95)	613	13680
9	G70-14/two-ply (four-ply rating) OE White Stripe (n.c.)	1,299	13680
4	F70-14/B Fiberglass Belt White Stripe** ($26.25)	5,127	13427-37-13637-67
5	F70-14/B Fiberglass Belt Red Stripe** ($26.25)	1,518	13427-37-13637-67
7	G70-14/B Fiberglass Red Stripe** ($25.95)	257	13680
0	Heavy Duty Battery	26,795	All
1	Map Lamp	34,113	All
4	Instrument Panel Gauges***	24,852	All
5	Speed Warning Indicator	4,372	All
5	Luggage Compartment Lamp	28,100	13427-37-13637-67
6	Underhood Lamp	34,114	All
8	Ash Tray Lamp	34,114	All
9	Instrument Panel Courtesy Lights	32,901	13427-37-13637-80
5	Electric Clock	75,277	All
6	Lamp Monitoring	2,041	13427-37-13637-67
7	Tape Player	12,635	13427-37-13637-67
3	Radio – Push Button	428,294	All
9	Radio – AM/FM Push Button	15,084	All
3	Manual Rear Antenna (N/A with U69)	33,117	13427-37-13637-67
9	Stereo Equipment	3,247	13427-37-13637-67
0	Auxiliary Speaker	64,165	13427-37-13637-67
1	Heavy Duty Radiator (included with AC or L78)	8,588	All
1	Front Bumper Guard	27,003	All
2	Rear Bumper Guard	19,543	13427-37-13637-67
5	Traction Compound & Dispenser	278	All
9	Auxiliary Lighting Group	34,116	All
3	Deluxe Seat Belts & Front Seat Shoulder Harness	48,792	13427-37-13637-80
5	SS 396 Equipment	86,307	All
X	Trim – Vinyl Coated Bench Seat****	220,594	13427-37-13637
5	SS 396 Paint (Monoco/Hugger Orange)	5,194	–
7	SS 396 Paint Yellow	2,841	All
9	Two-Tone Color Combination	21,690	13427-37-13637

Many options were available on non-SS 396 Equipment–optioned Chevelles, so the numbers in the Sold column are not necessarily SS 396 Equipment sales numbers.

"All" indicates all five possible SS 396 Equipment bodystyles.

*Standard equipment with SS 396 Equipment option.

**Standard versus optional tires is a bit tricky with the SS 396 Equipment option. On the coupe, sport coupes, and convertibles, an F70-14/two-ply (four-ply rating) white-lettered blackwall tire was standard; on the sedan pickup a G70-14/two-ply (four-ply rating) red-stripe tire was standard. Other tires were optional at either no cost or $26.95 on the coupe, sport coupes, and convertibles or $25.95 on the sedan pickup. Those shown as "OE" are no-cost optional tires with the SS 396 Equipment option and were optional on non-SS 396 Equipment–optioned Chevelles as well.

***Only available with the 13427-37 when Z25 ordered.

****RPO code is dependent on the color but will match Fisher Body Number Plate trim code.

*****Hideaway wipers were an option on 13427 and 13437 300 Deluxe series with or without SS 396 Equipment option. It is not known how many of the 706 reported sold were sold with the SS 396 Equipment option.

HOW MANY?

Questions are often asked such as, "How many LeMans Blue L34 convertibles were built?" or "How many L78 300 Deluxe sport coupes were built?" Unfortunately, unless one could find build records on every SS 396 Equipment–optioned Chevelle from the United States and Canada, there is no way of knowing. To date, there are no known surviving records to determine the, "How many . . ." question.

There are known production figures for particular series/bodystyles but not for how many were painted a particular color, how many were SS 396 Equipment optioned, and in many cases how many were equipped with a particular option. While there are known production figures for such options as the RPO Z25 SS 396 Equipment option, the option was available in five different series/bodystyle combinations. The problem of, "How many . . ." gets more complicated with combinations of options, such as, "How many of an option that could be ordered with and without the SS 396 Equipment option, such as air-conditioning, bucket seats, an M20 4-speed transmission, etc.?"

Take the RPO M20 4-speed transmission as an example. There were three different 4-speed transmissions sold under RPO M20. One was a cast-iron Saginaw used behind the 307-ci

V-8 engine with a 2.85:1 low gear, a second cast-iron Saginaw was used behind the 250-hp 350-ci engine with a 2.54:1 low gear, and the third was an aluminum-case Muncie used behind the 300-hp 350-ci engine and the L35 396-ci engine with a 2.52:1 low gear. All were ordered under RPO M20, but the particular engine dictated which of the three M20 transmissions the car would receive.

Probability Distribution

Trying to calculate how many of any particular engine (or any other option) that was used in any series/bodystyle can be tricky. You can calculate an evenly proportional distribution of certain equipment to a particular series/bodystyle.

For example, the SS 396 Equipment option was available in five different series/bodystyle combinations in the US. Canadian figures are not included here for several reasons: no L78s were built in Canada, no sedan pickups were built in Canada, and Vintage Vehicle Services can tell you how many of a particular engine were installed in the remaining series/bodystyles.

Canada did not build 1969 Chevelles with the RPO L78 engine option. All L78 Chevelles were imported into Canada for Canadian dealers and were generally built at the Baltimore, Maryland, assembly plant because it was the closest US plant.

It is known how many of each series/bodystyle was produced, and it is known how many SS 396 Equipment options were sold. There were 275,334 V-8 Malibu-series sport coupes built, 7,922 V-8 Malibu convertibles, 39,000 Malibu series sedan pickups, 5,259 300 Deluxe coupes, and 6,793 300 Deluxe sport coupes. In total 334,408 1969 Chevelles built in the US were candidates for the SS 396 Equipment option.

By taking the number built of any given series/bodystyle and the total number possible, one can calculate a percentage of that series/bodystyle against the total. For example, the 275,334 V-8 Malibu sport coupes account for 82.35 percent of the total of 334,408. Assuming an even distribution of SS 396 Equipment options sold (86,307), this calculates to 71,074 V-8 Malibu sport coupes being SS 396 Equipment optioned.

One caveat: it is not known if the 86,307 SS Equipment option figure includes Canadian sales. For consistency, these

Although there are no known production numbers on RPO L78 optioned Malibu convertibles, one can assume they are pretty scarce in the 1969 SS 396 world. (Photo Courtesy L78 Registry)

figures assume it does not. And here is where the rub comes in: not having separate production figures for US and Canada severely clouds calculations. If one assumes the 86,307 SS 396 Equipment options sold includes Canada, then one would have to add the number of each series/bodystyle imported from Canada. It can get quite messy from here, so you see why a claim such as, ". . . 1 of xxx L34 convertibles built . . ." is nothing more than a guess for a US-built Chevelle.

SS 396 Options Sold

Series/Bodystyle	Qty Sold (US)	Percentage	Possibilities
13427	5,259	1.57%	1,355
13437	6,793	2.03%	1,752
13637	275,334	82.35%	71,074
13667	7,922	2.36%	2,037
13680	39,000	11.66%	10,063
Total	334,308	100.00%	86,307

Now, think about distribution of other options, such as engines, transmissions, etc., and you can see the silliness one can get into.

One can do essentially the same thing by assembly plant. Given the General Motors production figures for each US assembly plant versus the number of RPO Z25 SS options, one can calculate an even distribution of SS Equipment–optioned Chevelles for each plant.

Plant	Production	Percentage SS	Possibilities
Atlanta	56,386	11.55%	9,968
Baltimore	114,385	23.43%	20,222
Framingham	67,942	13.92%	12,014
Fremont	68,119	13.95%	12,040
Kansas City	181,164	37.12%	32,037
Total	487,996	99.97%	86,281

Date:	February 3, 2017
Vehicle Identification Number:	1363791101█
Customer:	█████
Vehicle:	1969 Chevrolet Chevelle SS 396
Trim:	788 – Red Vinyl Strato Bucket Seats
Paint:	50 – Dover White
Top:	2B – Black
Stripe:	Red
Production Plant:	Oshawa, Ontario, Canada
Production Date:	September 18, 1968
Shipping Date:	September 24, 1968
Model Number:	13637 – Malibu – 2dr sport coupe
Engine:	396 CID 350 HP 4bbl Turbo Jet V8
Engine Number:	T0830JC
Dealer:	General Supplies Company Ltd. Calgary, Alberta, Canada
Number Produced For Sale In Canada (Same Model Number Only)	9, 612 (903 with Z/25; 294 with L/34)

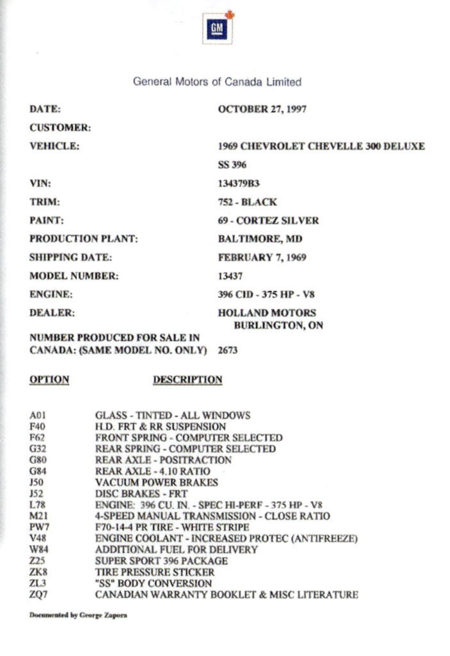

General Motors of Canada Limited

DATE:	OCTOBER 27, 1997
CUSTOMER:	
VEHICLE:	1969 CHEVROLET CHEVELLE 300 DELUXE SS 396
VIN:	134379B3
TRIM:	752 - BLACK
PAINT:	69 - CORTEZ SILVER
PRODUCTION PLANT:	BALTIMORE, MD
SHIPPING DATE:	FEBRUARY 7, 1969
MODEL NUMBER:	13437
ENGINE:	396 CID - 375 HP - V8
DEALER:	HOLLAND MOTORS BURLINGTON, ON
NUMBER PRODUCED FOR SALE IN CANADA: (SAME MODEL NO. ONLY)	2673

OPTION	DESCRIPTION
A01	GLASS - TINTED - ALL WINDOWS
F40	H.D. FRT & RR SUSPENSION
F62	FRONT SPRING - COMPUTER SELECTED
G32	REAR SPRING - COMPUTER SELECTED
G80	REAR AXLE - POSITRACTION
G84	REAR AXLE - 4.10 RATIO
J50	VACUUM POWER BRAKES
J52	DISC BRAKES - FRT
L78	ENGINE: 396 CU. IN. - SPEC HI-PERF - 375 HP - V8
M21	4-SPEED MANUAL TRANSMISSION - CLOSE RATIO
PW7	F70-14-4 PR TIRE - WHITE STRIPE
V48	ENGINE COOLANT - INCREASED PROTEC (ANTIFREEZE)
W84	ADDITIONAL FUEL FOR DELIVERY
Z25	SUPER SPORT 396 PACKAGE
ZK8	TIRE PRESSURE STICKER
ZL3	"SS" BODY CONVERSION
ZQ7	CANADIAN WARRANTY BOOKLET & MISC LITERATURE

Documented by George Zapora

1908 Colonel Sam Drive, Oshawa, Ontario L1H 8P7

The RPO L78 engine was not installed in any Canada-built Chevelle. This Vintage Vehicle Services report shows Baltimore as the production plant for this 300 Deluxe sport coupe. (Photo Courtesy L78 Registry)

Vintage Vehicle Services of Canada can supply documentation on any 1969 Chevelle either built in Canada or imported from the United States for sale by a Canadian dealer. This early model year Malibu sport coupe built on September 18, 1968, shows the VIN sequence starting with 100001 instead of the normal 300001. (Photo Courtesy SS 396 Registry)

This table should be taken with a larger dose of salt than normal for several reasons because Atlanta did not build convertibles or sedan pickups, and Framingham and Fremont did not build sedan pickups either, so these three plants would need to bolster their calculated SS production to the three remaining series/bodystyles.

The Oshawa, Ontario, plant in Canada is not included in the above table because Canada has known figures for RPO L35 and RPO L34 sales, hence a known number of these cars. Documentation from Vintage Vehicle Services in Oshawa has two categories, those built in and for sale in Canada (including those imported from the US) and those built in Canada for US sales, and those imported into Canada from the US. The Oshawa plant did not build the sedan pickup, and it did not install any RPO L78 engines in any 1969 Chevelle. While there are no documented figures on 1969 RPO L78 engine sales in Canada, it is known that several were imported for Canada sales.

Figures currently available for Oshawa are confusing and conflicting by the reports. Some reports are quite old (20 years), and figures conflict with newer reports.

The first table is for 1969 Chevelles built for Canadian dealer sales; the second is for 1969 Chevelles built in Canada for US dealer sales. For the blank cells, there are no known numbers as of this printing.

Series/Bodystyle	With L35	With L34
13427	36 (1)	
13437	36 (1)	
13637	136 (2)	294
13637 (3)	427	
13667	26	

(1) The number 36 includes both the 300 Deluxe coupe and 300 Deluxe sport coupe. (2) Number reported on late documentation for Chevelles produced for sale in Canada. (3) Number reported on old documentation.

It is interesting to note that the Vintage Vehicle Services documentation shows 903 13637 Malibu sport coupes were ordered with the RPO Z25 option, but figures for RPO L35 (146) and RPO L34 (294) engines are nowhere close to that with a total of only 440 accounted for.